CHARLES VANCE

PLC Ladder Logic fundamentals

A Guide to Understanding PLC Programming

First edition

This book was professionally typeset on Reedsy.
Find out more at reedsy.com

Contents

1

Introduction

A Programmable Logic Controller (PLC) is a special headless computer used in industrial environments to control and automate processes and machinery. It is designed to operate in harsh conditions based on programmed logic, monitoring inputs, making decisions, and controlling outputs to improve operations.

PLCs replace traditional relay-based control systems offering advantages such as automation of complex tasks, adaptability to changing requirements, reliability in harsh conditions, real-time control, centralized management, fault detection, safety features, cost-effectiveness, and integration with other control systems.

PLCs play a crucial role in various industries, enhancing productivity and efficiency through automated processes. Their versatility and ability to improve industrial automation have made them indispensable components in manufacturing, process control, automotive, energy, and other sectors.

Advantages of PLC versus Relays

PLCs are programmable. This flexibility allows quick adjustments to accommodate changes in production requirements without completely rewiring the control panel.

Another advantage is that PLC wiring is much less complicated than wiring required for relay logic. Also, PLC modules take up less real estate on the backplane of the control panel, the reduction in wiring and other hardware equals substantial cost savings in labor and material.

Using PLCs instead of relays also makes it possible to monitor registers and bit states in real-time; relays aren't intelligent and cannot be connected to computers—the capability of connecting to an HMI for a graphical display of the process or equipment operations is of tremendous benefit allowing operators to "see" what's going on in the process or equipment as its happening and observe control graphics to alert them to situations requiring immediate attention.

Troubleshooting is also much easier with a PLC, built-in diagnostics, and the ability to visualize the state of each instruction makes troubleshooting simple by comparison to the relay. Relay circuits consisted of hardwired contacts that often failed when dirty or "sticky" due to wear over time would create false signals an unexpected operation, these issued required time-consuming inspection techniques to discover and resolve.

These are only a few of the many advantages PLCs have over the traditional relay for control circuits. Relays continue to be used today, but are most commonly used for power handling and motor control rather than logic.

Common Applications for PLCs

PLCs are reliable, flexible and efficient and are widely used across all industries to automate processes and machinery.

In manufacturing PLCs are used to manage assembly lines, monitor and control equipment, and optimize production schedules, and are capable of simultaneous handling of many complex and intricate tasks improving quality and productivity.

In process control industries such as chemical, oil and gas or pharmaceuticals PLCs are used to monitor and control pressures, temperatures and flows with pinpoint accuracy. This ability to closely regulate critical processes ensures safe and efficient production.

Building automation is another area where PLCs are extensively used. They control heating, ventilation, and air conditioning (HVAC) systems, lighting, and security systems in commercial and residential buildings. PLCs contribute to energy efficiency by adjusting HVAC systems based on occupancy and environmental conditions, resulting in optimized energy consumption.

In the automotive industry, PLCs are essential for managing various manufacturing processes, including body assembly, painting, and welding. They coordinate the robotic systems responsible for assembly tasks, ensuring precise and synchronized movements, which are critical to maintaining quality and production efficiency.

PLCs also find applications in the food and beverage industry. They regulate and optimize processes in food processing plants, ensuring consistency in food production and adhering to stringent safety and hygiene standards. PLCs control tasks like mixing, baking, filling, and packaging, enabling efficient and safe food production.

The water and wastewater treatment sector relies on PLCs for monitoring and controlling treatment processes. PLCs manage the flow of water, monitor water quality parameters, and control the dosage of chemicals for treatment purposes. This ensures effective water purification and wastewater treatment, maintaining environmental standards.

In the power generation and distribution industry, PLCs are utilized for managing power grids, controlling substations, and optimizing electricity distribution. PLCs play a vital role in power system automation, helping to minimize downtime, improve fault detection, and enhance overall grid efficiency.

PLCs are extensively employed in material handling and logistics applications. They automate conveyor systems, sorters, and robotic arms in warehouses and distribution centers, facilitating smooth and efficient movement of goods, reducing manual labor, and minimizing errors.

These are just a few examples of the numerous applications of PLCs in various industries. As technology advances, the scope of PLC applications continues to grow, demonstrating the importance of these powerful control devices in shaping the future of automation and industrial processes.

2

Basic Components of PLC Systems

PLC (Programmable Logic Controller) hardware is a critical component in industrial automation systems. It consists of various physical components that work together to control and automate processes and machinery. Below is an overview of the essential hardware components found in a typical PLC system:

Central Processing Unit (CPU):

The CPU is the core component of a PLC and serves as its "brain." It is responsible for processing the control program, managing data, and executing the logic to control and automate industrial processes.

The CPU interprets the ladder logic, function block diagrams, or other programming languages used in the PLC and converts them into control actions. It scans the program repeatedly in a continuous loop, checking the status of inputs, executing the logic based on the programmed instructions, and updating the status of outputs accordingly.

The CPU's processing power and speed are crucial factors in determining the performance and responsiveness of the PLC. More powerful CPUs can handle complex logic and larger programs, allowing for more extensive control and monitoring capabilities.

Modern PLC CPUs often come equipped with multiple communication ports, enabling seamless integration with other devices and control systems. This connectivity facilitates data exchange and enables PLCs to be part of a larger networked automation system.

Additionally, some advanced PLC CPUs may have built-in features such as real-time clocks, battery backup to retain memory during power outages, and the ability to handle complex mathematical calculations for advanced control algorithms.

As PLC technology continues to evolve, the capabilities of CPUs are expanding, enabling PLCs to tackle increasingly complex automation tasks in various industries, including manufacturing, process control, automotive, energy, and more.

Input Modules:

Input modules are an integral part of a PLC system, responsible for interfacing with various sensors, switches, and devices that provide information about the state of the industrial process. These modules convert physical signals from the field devices into digital signals that the CPU can understand and process.

Input modules come in different configurations to accommodate various types of input signals. Common types of input modules include:

- **Digital Input Modules:** These modules handle discrete signals, representing binary states such as ON/OFF or HIGH/LOW. They are used to interface with devices like limit switches, push buttons, proximity sensors, and other devices that provide simple ON/OFF status information.
- **Analog Input Modules:** Analog input modules handle continuous signals, representing varying levels of a physical quantity, such as temperature, pressure, or voltage. They convert analog signals from sensors and transducers into digital values that the PLC can interpret and use for precise control and monitoring.
- **Specialized Input Modules:** Some PLC systems may require specialized input modules to interface with specific types of sensors such as RTD or

unique signal requirements. For instance, high-speed input modules can handle rapidly changing input signals, ideal for applications like motor speed feedback or encoder signals.

Input modules are typically mounted on the PLC's input rack and are connected to field devices through wiring terminals or connectors. The number and type of input modules used in a PLC system depend on the complexity and specific needs of the automation process.

During the PLC's scan cycle, the CPU reads the input status from the input modules and updates the corresponding memory locations. These inputs are then used by the PLC's control program to make decisions and execute the desired control actions based on the programmed logic.

The reliability and accuracy of input modules are critical for the overall performance of the PLC system. Robust input modules ensure that the PLC receives accurate and timely information from the field, enabling precise control and efficient automation of industrial processes.

Output Modules:

Output modules are essential components , responsible for interfacing with actuators, motors, solenoids, and other devices that control the industrial process. These modules convert digital signals from the CPU into physical control signals to actuate the output devices and bring about the desired changes in the process.

Like input modules, output modules come in various configurations to accommodate different types of output signals. Common types of output modules include:

- **Digital Output Modules:** These modules handle discrete output signals, typically representing binary states such as ON/OFF or HIGH/LOW. They are used to control devices like motors, relays, solenoid valves, and other devices that require simple binary control.
- **Analog Output Modules:** Analog output modules handle continuous

control signals, providing varying voltage or current levels to drive actuators with proportional control requirements. These modules are used for precise control of devices like variable speed drives, proportional valves, or motor speed controllers.

· **Specialized Output Modules:** In some cases, PLC systems may require specialized output modules to interface with specific devices or unique control requirements. For instance, high-speed output modules are used for applications that demand rapid and precise control actions, such as high-frequency pulse generation.

Output modules are typically mounted on the PLC's output rack and are connected to the field devices through wiring terminals or connectors. The CPU writes the appropriate control signals to the output modules' memory locations during its scan cycle. The output modules then convert these digital signals into physical control signals, activating or deactivating the connected devices as per the control program's instructions.

The reliability and accuracy of output modules are crucial to ensure the proper functioning of the industrial process. Robust output modules guarantee that the PLC can effectively control the actuators and devices, enabling the automation system to carry out the desired actions accurately and efficiently.

In summary, output modules play a vital role in PLC systems by interfacing with actuators and devices to control industrial processes. They enable the PLC to execute precise control actions based on the programmed logic, contributing to the automation and optimization of various applications in industries such as manufacturing, process control, and more.

Power Supply Unit (PSU):

The Power Supply Unit (PSU) is a critical component, responsible for providing the electrical power required to operate the PLC and its associated modules and devices.

PLCs typically operate on low-voltage DC power, which is supplied by the PSU. The PSU converts the incoming AC power from the mains into the appropriate DC voltage and current levels needed to power the CPU, input modules, output modules, communication modules, and other components of the PLC system.

The reliability and stability of the PSU are crucial for the overall performance and operation of the PLC. A stable power supply ensures that the PLC operates consistently and reliably, minimizing the risk of system failures and unexpected downtime.

In addition to providing power, some modern PLC PSUs offer additional features to enhance system functionality and safety. These features may include:

- **Redundancy:** Some PLC systems employ redundant power supplies to ensure continuous operation in the event of a PSU failure. Redundant power supplies can switch seamlessly between primary and backup power sources, preventing disruptions to critical processes.
- **Battery Backup:** Many PLC PSUs have built-in batteries or capacitors that provide backup power during brief power outages. This backup power allows the PLC to retain critical data, such as the control program and system configurations, ensuring a smooth resumption of operations once power is restored.
- **Overvoltage and Overcurrent Protection:** The PSU may include protection mechanisms to safeguard the PLC system from overvoltage and overcurrent conditions. These protection features prevent damage to the PLC components and ensure the system's safe operation.
- **Diagnostic and Status Indicators:** Some PSUs have diagnostic LEDs or status indicators that provide information about the PSU's health and status. This feature aids in troubleshooting and identifying potential PSU issues.

The PSU's specifications, such as input voltage range, output voltage, current ratings, and efficiency, are chosen based on the specific requirements of the PLC system. Proper sizing and selection of the PSU are essential to ensure that it can supply adequate power to all the components in the PLC system under maximum load conditions.

Overall, the PSU is a fundamental component of a PLC system, ensuring reliable and stable power supply to support the automation and control of industrial processes. Its design and features play a crucial role in maintaining the PLC's functionality, performance, and safety.

Communication Modules:

Communication modules are integral components that enable the exchange of data and information between the PLC and other devices, control systems, or networks. These modules provide connectivity, facilitating seamless integration of the PLC into larger automation systems and allowing for efficient data sharing and remote control.

PLCs equipped with communication modules can communicate using various protocols, depending on the specific requirements of the application and the devices involved. Some common communication protocols supported by communication modules include:

- **Ethernet:** Ethernet communication modules allow the PLC to communicate over standard Ethernet networks, making it possible to exchange data with other PLCs, Human-Machine Interfaces (HMIs), Supervisory Control and Data Acquisition (SCADA) systems, and other networked devices.
- **RS-232/RS-485:** RS-232 and RS-485 communication modules enable serial communication between the PLC and devices with serial interfaces, such as printers, barcode scanners, and other peripherals.
- **Fieldbus Protocols:** Communication modules may support various fieldbus protocols, such as Profibus, Modbus, DeviceNet, and CANopen, among others. These protocols are commonly used in industrial automation to connect PLCs with distributed I/O devices, sensors, and actuators.
- **Industrial Ethernet Protocols:** Some PLCs support industrial Ethernet protocols, such as Profinet, EtherNet/IP, and Modbus TCP, designed for real-time control and communication in industrial environments.
- **Wireless Communication:** Advanced PLC systems may feature wireless

communication modules that enable wireless data transmission, allowing for greater flexibility in device placement and communication in areas with challenging cabling requirements.

Communication modules facilitate data exchange in both directions, allowing the PLC to receive information from remote devices, process it, and send control commands or status updates back to those devices. This bidirectional communication enables real-time monitoring, remote control, and coordination of distributed processes.

The ability to communicate with other devices and systems enhances the capabilities of the PLC, enabling it to be part of complex automation solutions and Industrial Internet of Things (IIoT) architectures. Communication modules play a vital role in integrating the PLC with the broader industrial ecosystem, enhancing efficiency, and enabling data-driven decision-making.

The selection of the appropriate communication modules depends on the communication requirements, the devices to be integrated, and the overall system architecture. PLCs with robust communication capabilities are essential for modern industrial automation, allowing for seamless data flow and efficient coordination of interconnected devices and processes.

Memory:

Memory is a fundamental component of the PLC, crucial for storing the control program, data, and system parameters required for the PLC's operation. The memory in a PLC can be divided into two main types: Program Memory and Data Memory.

Program Memory:

Program Memory, also known as "RAM" (Random Access Memory) or "Working Memory," is where the PLC stores the control program. The control program consists of the ladder logic, function block diagrams, or other programming languages used to define the logic and behavior of the

PLC.

The program memory is volatile, meaning its contents are lost when the PLC loses power. As a result, the control program must be reloaded into the PLC's memory each time it is powered up. The PLC's CPU repeatedly scans the control program stored in program memory during its execution cycle. It reads the inputs, processes the logic based on the programmed instructions, and updates the outputs accordingly. The speed and efficiency of the PLC's scanning process are critical for achieving real-time control of industrial processes.

Data Memory:

Also known as "EEPROM" (Electrically Erasable Programmable Read-Only Memory) or "Non-volatile Memory," is used to store data and system parameters that need to be retained even when the PLC loses power. Unlike program memory, data memory is non-volatile, allowing the PLC to preserve data across power cycles.

Data memory stores various types of information, such as system configurations, user-defined parameters, I/O status, and intermediate data used during program execution. Examples of data stored in memory include setpoints, counter values, timer values, and other temporary data required for control actions.

The size of the memory in a PLC system depends on the complexity of the control program and the amount of data that needs to be stored. PLCs used in larger and more complex applications generally have more significant memory capacities to accommodate extensive programs and data requirements.

Maintaining the integrity of the data in memory is critical for the PLC's reliability and performance. PLCs may have backup mechanisms, such as battery backup or capacitor backup, to ensure that data stored in data memory is preserved during brief power outages, allowing for a smooth resumption of operations when power is restored.

Backplane:

The backplane is a critical component of the PLC system, serving as a physical structure that facilitates the interconnection of various modules within the PLC. It provides a communication pathway that allows the CPU, input modules, output modules, communication modules, and other components to exchange data and signals seamlessly.

The backplane is typically a printed circuit board (PCB) with multiple slots designed to accommodate the different modules used in the PLC system. These modules plug directly into the slots on the backplane, forming a secure and reliable connection.

Each module inserted into the backplane is designed to perform specific functions, such as processing inputs, generating outputs, or handling communication tasks. The backplane ensures that all these modules can communicate with the CPU and each other effectively.

The backplane acts as a central hub, providing electrical power and data connections between the modules. The power supply unit (PSU) delivers power to the backplane, which then distributes power to all the connected modules, including the CPU and I/O modules.

In addition to power distribution, the backplane facilitates the transfer of input data from the input modules to the CPU for processing. Similarly, it enables the transmission of output data from the CPU to the output modules, which control actuators and devices in the industrial process.

One significant advantage of the backplane design is its modularity. PLC systems can be easily customized and expanded by adding or removing modules from the backplane. This modularity allows for flexible configurations, enabling users to adapt the PLC system to the specific needs of their automation application.

Furthermore, the backplane enhances the reliability of the PLC system. The direct connection between modules and the backplane reduces wiring complexity, minimizing the chances of loose connections or wiring errors. This streamlined design improves system integrity and reduces the potential for failures.

PLC Software Overview:

PLC software is a crucial element of a Programmable Logic Controller (PLC) system, responsible for programming and configuring the PLC to control industrial processes. The software provides a user-friendly interface that allows engineers, programmers, and operators to create, edit, and manage the PLC's control logic and functionality.

Here is an overview of the key aspects and functionalities of PLC software:

Programming Environment:

PLC software typically provides a programming environment where users can write and edit the control program supporting IEC 61131-3 standard consisting of various programming languages, such as ladder logic, function block diagrams (FBD), structured text (ST), instruction list (IL), and sequential function charts (SFC).

- **Ladder Logic Editor:** Ladder logic is one of the most widely used programming languages in PLCs. The software includes a ladder logic editor that allows users to create ladder diagrams by arranging logical and arithmetic functions in a graphical manner, resembling traditional relay logic diagrams.
- **Function Block Diagram Editor:** For users who prefer a graphical representation of control functions, the software may include a function block diagram editor. Function blocks represent functional units that perform specific operations and can be interconnected to create control logic.
- **Structured Text Editor:** For more advanced programming tasks, PLC software often provides a structured text editor. Structured text is a high-level programming language similar to programming languages used in software development, enabling complex control algorithms and mathematical computations.
- **Project Management:** PLC software allows users to organize their projects efficiently. Users can create and manage multiple projects, each contain-

ing the associated control program, configuration settings, and data.

- **Communication Configuration:** The software includes tools for configuring communication settings to establish connections between the PLC and external devices, Human-Machine Interfaces (HMIs), Supervisory Control and Data Acquisition (SCADA) systems, and other networked devices.

- **Simulation and Testing:** PLC software often provides simulation capabilities, allowing users to test and debug the control program without physically connecting to the PLC hardware. Simulation enables engineers to validate the logic and verify the expected behavior before deploying the program to the PLC.

- **Download and Upload Functionality:** PLC software allows users to download the control program from the software to the PLC's memory for execution. Conversely, users can upload the control program from the PLC to the software, facilitating backup, documentation, and version control.

- **Diagnostics and Monitoring:** The software may include diagnostic tools to monitor the PLC's status, I/O states, and system performance in real-time. Diagnostics aid in troubleshooting and identifying issues for timely resolution.

- **Security Features:** To ensure the integrity and security of the control program, PLC software often includes features for password protection, access control, and data encryption.

PLC software is a powerful tool that empowers engineers and programmers to design sophisticated control strategies, automate industrial processes, and optimize system performance. Its user-friendly interface and diverse programming options make it accessible to users with varying levels of expertise, supporting the development of efficient and reliable automation solutions.

3

PLC Programming Fundamentals

Ladder Logic Programming is a graphical language widely used in PLCs for industrial automation. It visually resembles traditional relay logic diagrams, with control logic represented using ladder rungs. Each rung specifies a control condition or operation, scanned sequentially from top to bottom to execute control actions based on the specified conditions.

In Ladder Logic, contacts and coils are the main elements. Contacts represent input conditions like switches or sensors and can be normally open (NO) or normally closed (NC). Coils represent output actions, such as turning on or off a motor or relay. The arrangement of contacts and coils in a rung determines the control logic.

Ladder Logic supports basic logic operations like AND, OR, NOT, and NAND. These operations are used to create complex control conditions by combining multiple contacts in series or parallel.

A ladder rung is activated when all the contacts in a series are true (energized) or when any of the contacts in a parallel branch are true, representing logical AND and OR operations, respectively.

Ladder Logic allows for feedback and memory elements, such as latches (SET/RESET coils) and timers. These elements enable the control system to "remember" past states and introduce time-based delays and actions.

The PLC executes the Ladder Logic program in a continuous loop called the scan cycle. During each cycle, the PLC scans all rungs from top to bottom, evaluating the logic conditions and updating the output coils accordingly.

Ladder Logic programming is popular due to its simplicity, visual representation, and similarity to traditional relay logic. Engineers and programmers familiar with electrical circuits find it easy to understand, making it a preferred choice for automating complex industrial processes and machinery.

Symbols and Basic Instructions (Contacts, Coils, Timers, Counters)

Symbols and Basic Instructions are fundamental elements in Ladder Logic Programming, representing the building blocks for creating control logic in Programmable Logic Controllers (PLCs). These elements include Contacts, Coils, Timers, and Counters:

Contacts:

Contacts represent input conditions in the control logic. They can be either normally open (NO) or normally closed (NC) and are analogous to physical switches or sensors. NO contacts become "true" (energized) when the input condition is met, while NC contacts become "true" when the input condition is not met.

Input1   Input1

─┤ ├─   ─┤ / ├─

Coils:

Coils represent output actions in the control logic. They are used to control physical devices, such as motors, solenoids, or relays. When a coil is energized, the corresponding output device is activated, and when it is de-energized, the device is deactivated.

Output1

( )

Timers:

Timers are essential for introducing time delays in the control logic. They are used to control actions that should occur after a specified time duration has passed. Timers have a preset time value and can be either "ON-delay" or "OFF-delay," depending on whether the time delay is applied before or after the associated coil is energized. Three types of times are shown below, the TON timer that begins timing when the timer input transitions fro false to true, the TOF timer that begins timing when the timer input transitions from true to false, and the TP timer that generates a pulse the width of the preset every time the input transitions from false to true.

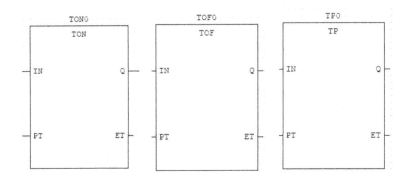

Counters:

Counters are used to count the occurrences of specific events or input conditions. They allow the PLC to keep track of the number of times an event has happened and can be used for various applications, such as counting products on a conveyor belt or tracking production cycles. Three main types of counters are the CTU, the CTD and the CTUD. The CTU counter increments when the input transitions false to true, the CTD counter decrements and the CTUD counter can both increment and decrement depending on which input transitions from false to true.

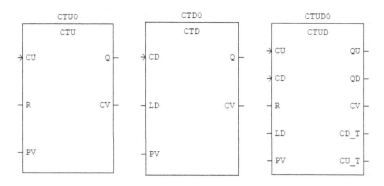

These basic instructions, along with logic operations like AND, OR, and NOT, provide a powerful toolkit for creating complex control strategies in Ladder Logic Programming. By combining contacts, coils, timers, and counters with logic operations, engineers and programmers can design efficient and precise control sequences to automate industrial processes effectively.

The symbols used to represent these basic instructions in Ladder Logic resemble electrical symbols used in circuit diagrams. Engineers and technicians can easily interpret and understand the logic flow by visually analyzing the ladder rungs, making Ladder Logic a preferred programming language in industrial automation due to its simplicity and visual representation.

Boolean Logic Operations

Boolean logic operations are fundamental logical operations used in computer programming, digital electronics, and PLC programming. They involve evaluating conditions and determining whether a statement is true or false (1 or 0, respectively). The three primary Boolean logic operations are AND, OR, and NOT.

AND Operation:

The AND operation evaluates two or more conditions and returns true (1) only if all the conditions are true (1). If any of the conditions are false (0), the AND operation returns false (0). In terms of truth tables, the AND operation can be represented as follows:

Input A	Input B	Output
0	0	0
0	1	0
1	0	0
1	1	1

OR Operation:

The OR operation evaluates two or more conditions and returns true (1) if at least one of the conditions is true (1). If all the conditions are false (0), the OR operation returns false (0). The truth table for the OR operation is as follows:

Input A	Input B	Output
0	0	0
0	1	1
1	0	1
1	1	1

NOT Operation:

The NOT operation (also known as inversion or negation) takes a single condition and returns the opposite value. If the input condition is true (1), the NOT operation returns false (0), and vice versa. The truth table for the NOT operation is as follows:

Input	Output
0	1
1	0

Boolean logic operations are the building blocks of logical expressions in programming and digital circuit design. They play a crucial role in decision-making, control flow, and data processing in various applications, including PLC programming for industrial automation. By combining these basic operations, more complex logical conditions can be constructed, enabling engineers and programmers to implement sophisticated control strategies and algorithms.

Input and Output Addressing

Input and output addressing are essential concepts in Programmable Logic Controllers (PLCs) that enable the interaction between the PLC and external devices, sensors, and actuators. These addressing methods allow the PLC to read input signals from the field and write output signals to control industrial processes.

Input Addressing:

Input addressing refers to the method used to identify and access the input signals connected to the PLC. Inputs can represent various field devices, such as switches, sensors, push buttons, or limit switches, providing information about the state of the process or machine. The input addressing method assigns a unique identifier or address to each input signal, allowing the PLC to monitor and process these signals.

Common input addressing methods include:

· **Discrete Input Addressing:** In this method, each input signal is assigned a specific address, usually represented by a binary number. For example, the first input might be addressed as I0, the second input as I1, and so on.
· **Word Input Addressing:** In some cases, multiple input signals can be grouped together into a word. The word address identifies the starting address of the group, and individual inputs within the word are accessed by specifying their bit position.

Output Addressing:

Output addressing refers to the method used to identify and access the output signals from the PLC to control external devices, actuators, or other equipment in the industrial process. Outputs can represent motors, solenoids, relays, or other devices that perform actions based on the control program's logic.

Similar to input addressing, output addressing methods include:

- **Discrete Output Addressing:** Each output signal is assigned a unique address, typically represented by a binary number. For instance, the first output might be addressed as Q0, the second output as Q1, and so forth.
- **Word Output Addressing:** Similar to input addressing, multiple output signals can be grouped together into a word. The word address identifies the starting address of the group, and individual outputs within the word are accessed by specifying their bit position.

Proper input and output addressing are crucial for ensuring accurate communication between the PLC and external devices. Engineers and programmers must configure the addressing correctly in the PLC's programming software to read input signals accurately and write control signals to the correct output devices. Accurate addressing is vital for reliable and precise control of industrial processes and machinery. Addressing structure varies widely between PLC type making it critical to consult configuration manuals and specifications provided by each manufacturer.

For the purpose of this book we will use the OpenPLC structure which provides an addressing scheme that can be configured across a wide array of controller hardware.

Openplc Addressing Structure

OpenPLC IO addressing uses a table format to configure inputs and outputs and assign each to a physical address on the target hardware. With proprietary PLC hardware such as Rockwell, Modicon, or others the IO addressing structure is fixed according to the internal physical addressing structure of that PLC. OpenPLC is a software soluiton that allows flexible IO assignment depending on the type of target device used. In this example I have used the Arduino UNO as the target hardware.

Arduino UNO Physical Addressing

IO TYPE	PIN NUMBER	ADDRESS
Digital In	2,3,4,5,6	%IX0.0-%IX0.4
Digital Out	7,8,12,13	%QX0.0-%QX0.3
Analog In	A0,A1,A2,A3,A4,A5	%IW0-%IW5
Analog Out	9,10,11	%QW0-%QW2

UNO Physical Address Table

#	Name	Class	Type	Location
1	Start	Local	BOOL	%IX0.0
2	Stop	Local	BOOL	%IX0.1
3	Aux	Local	BOOL	%IX0.2
4	Preset	Local	INT	%QW0
5	Accum	Local	INT	%IW0
6	Motor	Local	BOOL	%QX0.0

As each address is created using OpenPLC its type and physical location is assigned in the addressing table referencing the physical address of the target hardware device. Our ladder logic uses the value found in the name field that is aliased to the physical address based on the table values, later if we choose to use a different hardware platform all that is needed is to modify the value in the location column to match the new hardware. No changes would be required in the existing ladder logic.

Creating a Simple Ladder Logic Program

Let's create a simple Ladder Logic program to control the operation of a motor based on two input conditions: a start button and a stop button. The motor should turn on when the start button is pressed and turn off when the stop button is pressed.

Assumptions:

- Start input is connected to the Start button (Normally Open contact).
- Stop input is connected to the Stop button (Normally Closed contact).
- Aux input is connected to motor running contact (Normally Open contact).
- Motor output is connected to the motor (Coil).

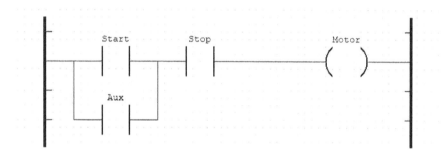

Explanation:

- The Start button (Start input) is represented by a Normally Open contact in the left most position of the rung. When the Start button is pressed (true), the contact becomes closed (1).
- The Stop button (Stop input) is represented by a Normally Closed contact to the right of the Start contact. When the Stop button is pressed (false), the contact becomes open (0).
- The Coil (Motor output) representing the motor is located in the right-most position on the rung. When the control logic allows the coil to be energized (1), the motor turns on, and when it is de-energized (0), the motor turns off.

- The Aux contact (Aux input) is represented by a Normally Open contact at the left and directly underneath the start input. When the motor contactor is energized the auxiliary contact will close (1).
- In the ladder rung, we have an AND operation and an OR operation. The motor will turn on only when both the Start button (Start input) and the Stop button (Stop input) are not pressed simultaneously (AND). Once the auxiliary contact closes the circuit will "seal" in and remain energized until the Stop button is pressed (OR).

Ladder Logic Operation:

- If the Start button is pressed (Start input = 1) and the Stop button is not pressed (Stop input = 1), the AND operation will evaluate to true (1).
- In this case, the output coil (Motor output) will be energized (1), and the motor will turn on.
- Once the motor contactor is energized the auxillary contact closes (Aux input = 1) and the motor circuit is sealed in.
- If either the Start button is not pressed (Start input = 0) or the Stop button is pressed (Stop input = 0), the AND operation will evaluate to false (0).
- In this case, the output coil (Motor output) will be de-energized (0), and the motor will turn off.

This simple Ladder Logic program demonstrates the basic control of a motor using three input conditions. The program can be expanded and modified to include additional control logic and more complex automation tasks, depending on the requirements of the specific industrial application.

Defining Project Requirements and Specifications

Defining the requirements and specifications is a crucial initial step in any engineering or development project, including those involving PLCs and industrial automation. Properly defining the requirements and specifications ensures that all stakeholders have a clear understanding of the project's objectives and scope, leading to successful and efficient project execution. Here's how to define requirements and specifications for a PLC automation project:

Understand the Project Scope:

Begin by understanding the overall scope of the project. Identify the processes, machinery, or systems that need automation and the specific tasks the PLC will be responsible for. Clarify the project's boundaries to avoid scope creep and ensure focus on the essential aspects. If it exists, use the project contract as a guide to set project boundaries and obligations, a great place to start is reading the original proposal documents, including the Request For Proposal (RFP) and any customer documentation that came with the RFP.

Next, thoroughly study any responses to the RFP incorporated into the contract, further flesh out the contours of the project scope, and may reveal areas of concern or possible technical issues related to final project fulfillment and customer satisfaction. Once the project scope is determined using the contract and supporting documentation, it is time to generate an equipment list and IO list.

Identify Stakeholders and Their Objectives:

If no contract exists, or this is an internal project without a contract, determine the key stakeholders involved, such as end-users, engineers, operators, and management. Understand their objectives, expectations, and requirements. Gather input from all stakeholders to ensure their needs are considered in the project's design and implementation. Small projects may have few or a single stakeholder, but it is essential to understand what is being asked for and develop specifications and lists that match the requirements.

Define Functional Requirements:

Clearly articulate the functional requirements the PLC system must meet. Writing a control narrative is a great way to define all of the functional requirements. Specify the inputs, outputs, control actions, and responses needed to achieve the desired automation. Describe the logical operations, timing, and sequencing required for the control logic. Define performance requirements, such as response times, cycle times, and processing speeds. Set timing constraints to ensure the PLC system meets the required performance levels for the specific application.

Specify Safety and Reliability Requirements:

If the PLC system controls critical or hazardous processes, define safety requirements and reliability criteria. Identify emergency stop procedures, fault handling mechanisms, and fail-safe features to ensure the safety of personnel and equipment. Usually, process engineers will develop a detailed cause-and-effect chart listing every process condition that requires operator intervention. Alarm thresholds and triggers are defined in such documents and provide an established guide for alarm rationalization and management.

Consider Environmental Conditions:

Take into account the operating environment of the PLC system. Consider factors such as temperature, humidity, vibration, and electromagnetic interference. Specify any special environmental protections or enclosures needed for the PLC hardware.

Address Communication and Integration:

If the PLC system needs to communicate with other devices, sensors, or systems, define the communication protocols and integration requirements. Ensure compatibility with existing control systems and data exchange standards. Developing a comprehensive equipment list provides insights into integration between system components, and this information will reveal potential interconnection issues, each equipment interconnect must be understood. If there are questions about how a particular piece of equipment or subsystem communicates, it's critical to determine the correct hardware interface to reveal the appropriate communication protocol. For example, if two components have RS-485 interface Modbus RTU is an appropriate protocol; however, if the components have ethernetModbusTCP protocol is a better choice.

Document User Interface Requirements:

If the PLC system includes an HMI, specify the user interface requirements. Define the layout, navigation, and visual elements needed for intuitive operation and monitoring. Process Instrumentation diagrams are useful to determine graphics needed to visualize the process.

Compliance and Standards:

Ensure that the PLC system complies with relevant industry standards, safety regulations, and code requirements. Adherence to these standards is essential for legal and regulatory compliance.

Document Traceability and Verification:

Clearly document all requirements and specifications to establish traceability throughout the project's lifecycle. Set up verification procedures to ensure that the PLC system meets the specified requirements. Good change management procedures will make sure that everyone that needs to know about a change is in the loop and eliminates mistakes that happen when multiple teams are working together and interacting in the same code base.

Translating Requirements into Ladder Logic Diagrams

Translating requirements into Ladder Logic Diagrams involves converting the functional requirements and specifications of the Programmable Logic Controller (PLC) system into a visual representation using ladder rungs. Here's a step-by-step guide to translating requirements into Ladder Logic Diagrams:

1. **Review Functional Requirements:** Start by reviewing the functional requirements and specifications you defined earlier. Make sure there is a clear understanding of the inputs, outputs, control actions, and logic operations required for the automation process. Process and Instrumentation Diagrams (P&IDs) are crucial to understanding functionality when working with process control.

2. **Identify Input and Output Addresses:** Assign unique addresses to each input and output used in the control logic. Use these addresses in the Ladder Logic Diagram to reference the corresponding physical inputs and outputs connected to the PLC. Confirm the equipment list includes every component of the project and use it to verify that the IO list matches all aspects of the equipment list. For example, if there are three motors listed requiring start/stop and auxiliary feedback contacts make sure each the IO list contains 9 digital inputs and 3 digital outputs. This way the two documents provide a cross check to highlight missing IO or equipment.

3. **Break Down the Control Logic:** Divide the control logic into manageable segments or rungs. Each rung should represent a specific control condition or operation. In our example for motor control, each motor will contain a seal-in circuit consisting of the start/stop, motor coil, and auxiliary seal-in input. If other equipment or functions added later are directly associated with each motor, place the new supporting logic rungs with the appropriate motor logic. Some PLCs allow subroutines and specialized instructions for more granular logic segregation according to function. Flow charts and logic diagrams are also helpful when determining required logic instructions.

4. **Choose Appropriate Ladder Logic Symbols:** Select the appropriate ladder

logic symbols (contacts and coils) to represent the input conditions and output actions in the control logic. Use normally open (NO) or normally closed (NC) contacts based on the logic requirements. Logic diagrams or flow charts reveal which type instruction is required to accomplish a particular function.

5. **Arrange the Ladder Rungs:** Organize the ladder rungs in a logical sequence based on the order of operations and control flow. The arrangement of rungs determines the order in which the PLC will evaluate the control conditions.

6. **Implement Logic Operations:** Use AND, OR, NOT, timers, and counters to implement the required logic operations. Combine contacts in series (AND operation) or parallel (OR operation) to create complex control conditions.

7. **Add Safety Interlocks:** If the project includes safety requirements, incorporate safety interlocks into the Ladder Logic Diagram. Ensure that the safety interlocks prevent hazardous operations and provide fail-safe mechanisms.

8. **Implement Timers and Counters:** If the project involves time-based or counting operations, add timers and counters to the Ladder Logic Diagram. Configure timers for ON-delay or OFF-delay operations as per the requirements.

9. **Add HMI and SCADA Integration (Optional):** If the PLC system includes an HMI or SCADA interface, incorporate the appropriate ladder logic elements to interact with the graphical user interface and display real-time data.

10. **Test and Verify:** Before deploying the Ladder Logic Diagram to the PLC, thoroughly test and verify the control logic. Use simulation tools in the PLC programming software to ensure that the logic behaves as expected and meets all requirements.

11. **Document and Comment:** Document the Ladder Logic Diagram with clear labels, comments, and descriptions. Properly document each rung and section of the diagram to enhance readability and understanding for future reference.

12. **Deploy the Ladder Logic:** Finally, download the Ladder Logic Diagram to the PLC hardware, allowing the controller to execute the programmed logic and control the automation process based on the defined requirements.

By following these steps, you can effectively translate functional requirements and specifications into Ladder Logic Diagrams, creating a clear and structured control logic for your PLC automation project.

Testing and Debugging the Program

Testing and debugging the program is critical in the PLC automation project. It ensures the Ladder Logic program functions as intended and meets all the specified requirements. Here are the key steps to test and debug the PLC program:

Start by performing offline testing using simulation tools available in the PLC programming software allowing verification of the logic functionality without connecting to the physical devices. Simulate various input scenarios to test the behavior of the control logic and check the output status to ensure that the coil actions execute appropriately.

Use step-by-step debugging features in the programming software to trace the program's execution line by line to identify potential issues and understand the program's flow. During the simulation, monitor critical variables, timers, counters, and memory addresses to verify their values and update rates.

Conduct functional testing to ensure that the PLC program achieves its intended purpose. Verify that the motor or equipment operates as expected and follows the desired control sequences. Test error handling mechanisms and verify that the program gracefully handles unexpected conditions.

After successful offline testing:

1. Deploy the program to the actual PLC hardware.
2. Conduct real-time testing with the physical inputs and outputs to ensure the program behaves as expected in the live environment.

3. Validate safety features and test safety interlocks to prevent hazardous situations.

Keep a log of any issues encountered during testing and the corresponding solutions. This documentation helps in future troubleshooting and maintenance. Involve operators and users in the testing process and gather their feedback on the program's functionality and ease of use.

Fine-tune the control logic based on the test results and user feedback if necessary. Iterate the testing and debugging process until the program operates flawlessly. Create a backup of the PLC program before deploying it to production to safeguard against unexpected issues.

Train operators and maintenance personnel how to operate the equipment, respond to alarms, and perform routine maintenance tasks. Continuous monitoring and periodic maintenance help maintain the program's performance over time.

By following these testing and debugging steps, you can ensure that the PLC program functions reliably, safely, and efficiently, meeting all the project requirements and specifications.

4

PLC Input and Output Module Devices

Analog and discrete field device types are essential components in industrial automation, enabling the exchange of information between the real-world processes and the control system. Each device type serves distinct purposes and interfaces with PLCs to monitor, measure, and control various physical parameters.

Digital Inputs (Push Buttons, Sensors)

Digital inputs are used to sense binary signals representing two states: ON (1) or OFF (0). These signals are typically generated by digital devices such as push buttons, limit switches, proximity sensors, and other types of sensors. Here's a closer look at digital inputs and some common examples:

Push Buttons:

Push buttons are momentary switches that are manually operated by pressing and releasing the button. They provide a simple way for operators or users to initiate specific actions in the control system. When the push button is pressed, the digital input associated with it becomes active (ON), and when the button is released, the input returns to an inactive state (OFF).

Normally open push buttons are typically used for start, reset, initiate, or other functions requiring momentary input decisions from an operator, normally closed buttons are used for stop buttons, emergency stop buttons or other safety related operator input where a wire break initiates the stop or emergency stop. If a normally open contact were used in these situations a wire break in the button would prevent the operator from stopping the equipment, using normally closed contacts provides a fail safe operation for these cases. Most industrial grade push button devices are equipped with both a normally open set and a normally closed set of contacts.

Multi-contact push buttons

Limit Switches:

Limit switches are mechanical switches used to detect the presence or absence of an object or to sense the position of moving parts in a machine. They have a lever or plunger that actuates the switch when it comes into contact with the target. When the limit switch is activated, the corresponding digital input is set to ON. Some typical uses of limit switches include travel limits on large motorized valves, home position for linear motion applications, float based level hard limits for Hi Hi or Lo Lo conditions, panel door closure and many others.

Industrial Limit Switch

Proximity Sensors:

Proximity sensors are non-contact devices used to detect the presence or absence of objects within their sensing range. They can be inductive, capacitive, ultrasonic, or photoelectric sensors. When an object enters the sensing area of a proximity sensor, the digital input linked to it is triggered to an ON state. Proximity sensors are great where the environment does not permit contact such as counting turns on a rotary device, or other moving parts where its necessary to know proximity of one part of the equipment to another.

Proximity Switch

Photoelectric Sensors:

Photoelectric sensors use light beams to detect objects and their properties, such as distance or color. They consist of an emitter and a receiver, and when an object interrupts the light beam, the receiver detects the change and sets the associated digital input to ON. Photo eyes are mostly used when a "fence" is needed to protect operators from entering a hazardous area or pinch point. PEs are also useful for detecting levels of materials that cannot otherwise be detected such as light materials such as rayon filling a bin.

Photo Eye

Magnetic Sensors:

Magnetic sensors detect changes in magnetic fields and are commonly used in applications where contact-based sensors might wear out or not be suitable. They are often used in door switches, security systems, or magnetic proximity sensors to detect the presence of ferrous materials.

Mag Switch

Reed Switches:

Reed switches are magnetic switches that use a pair of ferromagnetic reeds encapsulated within a glass tube. When a magnetic field is applied, the reeds attract, completing the electrical circuit and changing the state of the digital input.

Reed Switch

Microswitches:

Microswitches are small, sensitive switches with a spring-loaded lever. They are often used in safety interlocks, machine guarding, and limit detection applications. When the lever is actuated by a specific motion, the microswitch changes state, indicating the presence or absence of the motion.

Micro Switch

These digital inputs provide critical information to the PLC's control logic, allowing the system to respond to user inputs, monitor the status of various devices, and execute control actions based on the detected states. Proper configuration and reliable operation of digital inputs are essential for accurate and safe automation of industrial processes and machinery.

Digital Outputs (Relays, Solenoids, Pilot Lights)

Digital outputs in PLCs control binary devices or devices with two states: ON (energized) or OFF (de-energized). These digital outputs are commonly used to activate or deactivate external equipment, actuators, and indicators. Some of the typical examples of digital outputs in PLC systems are:

Relays:

Relays are electro-mechanical devices that use an electromagnetic coil to control one or more sets of contacts. When the digital output of the PLC energizes the relay coil, it creates a magnetic field that pulls the contacts together, completing the electrical circuit. This allows current to flow to the controlled device, such as a motor, lamp, or heating element. When the digital output de-energizes the relay coil, the contacts open, breaking the circuit and turning off the controlled device.

Motor Contactor, Ice Cube Relay, Solid State Relay

Solenoids:

Solenoids are electromagnetic devices that convert electrical energy into mechanical motion. When the digital output of the PLC energizes the solenoid coil, it creates a magnetic field that pulls a plunger or core inside the solenoid. This movement activates the mechanical action of the solenoid, such as opening or closing a valve, actuating a latch, or pushing or pulling a mechanism.

Solenoid

Pilot Lights:

Pilot lights, also known as indicator lights or signal lamps, are small visual indicators that provide status information to operators and users. They typically have a colored lens (red, green, yellow) to indicate different conditions. When the digital output of the PLC energizes the pilot light, it illuminates, providing a visual indication of the associated process or equipment status. For example, a green pilot light may indicate that a machine is running, while a red pilot light may indicate a fault or alarm condition.

Allen Bradley Pilot Light

These digital output devices - relays, solenoids, and pilot lights - are essential components for controlling and indicating the status of external devices in industrial automation and control systems. PLCs use digital outputs to execute control actions, drive actuators, and provide crucial feedback to operators for efficient and safe operation of industrial processes and machinery. Pilot lights for control panels have become rare in modern control systems design, the advent of HMI computers and SCADA systems with mobile graphic devices have all but eliminated the need to hard wired control panels.

Analog Inputs (Temperature, Pressure, Flow, Level, Current, Voltage)

Analog inputs are vital for monitoring and controlling various physical parameters in industrial automation. They enable the PLC to receive continuous and variable signals from different sensors, providing real-time data for precise control and monitoring. Here are common examples of analog inputs in PLCs:

Temperature Sensors:

Analog temperature sensors, such as thermocouples and resistance temperature detectors (RTDs), measure the temperature of the surrounding environment or specific components within a process. PLCs use these signals to monitor and regulate temperature-sensitive processes in industries like manufacturing, chemical processing, and HVAC systems. Both thermocouples and RTDs require specialty input modules designed specifically to handle the small signals each device generates. The physical appearance of each on is similar with the exception that thermocouples have two wires and RTDs have two, three, or four wire configurations available. RTDs are more accurate across the range of temperatures but thermocouples are capable of measuring much higher temperature extremes.

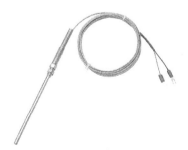

Thermocouple

Pressure Sensors:

Analog pressure sensors measure fluid pressure and convert it into an electrical output signal. They are widely used in pneumatic and hydraulic systems, as well as in various industrial processes, to monitor and control pressure levels. PLCs receive the analog pressure signals to ensure proper equipment functionality and maintain optimal pressure conditions. Two common pressure measurements are direct and differential pressure. Differential pressure transmitters are equipped with two ports while direct pressure transmitters have a single port, dual range transmitters have two ports that allow one port to be blocked for direct pressure applications.

4-20 mA Pressure Transmitter

Flow Rate Sensors:

Analog flow rate sensors measure the rate of fluid flow, such as liquids or gases, within a system. They provide continuous flow data, critical for process control and monitoring in industries like water treatment, oil and gas, and food processing. PLCs use these signals to adjust flow rates and optimize efficiency. Flow rates can be determined using various methods including differential pressure across a known orifice size, turbine based flow meters, or Magnetic, Coriolis,Vortex and Thermal flow meters. Each type meter has its own advantages and disadvantages with application requirements determining which is type is selected. The most common flow meter types are differential pressure and mag flow.

Turbine, Magnetic, Ultrasonic, and Coriolis flow meters

Level Sensors:

Analog level sensors measure the level of liquids or solids within containers or tanks. They provide continuous level data, allowing PLCs to monitor storage levels, control filling or emptying processes, and prevent overflow or underflow situations. Level sensors are widely used in industries such as chemical processing, food and beverage, and wastewater treatment. Level sensors are essential devices used to measure the level of liquids, solids, or slurries in containers, tanks, or vessels in various industrial applications. There are several methods for level measurement, each offering unique advantages and limitations.

Float level sensors use buoyant floats that move up and down with the liquid level, providing a simple and cost-effective solution for non-corrosive liquids and bulk solid level measurements. Ultrasonic level sensors utilize ultrasonic waves to measure the distance between the sensor and the liquid surface, making them suitable for non-contact measurement in open and closed vessels, regardless of liquid characteristics.

Pressure level sensors, also known as hydrostatic level sensors, accurately measure the liquid level based on the pressure exerted by the liquid's weight. They are versatile and can handle various liquids, including corrosive or viscous fluids. Capacitance level sensors measure the change in capacitance between the sensor probe and the liquid surface, making them suitable for both conductive and non-contact liquids, including challenging conditions or fouling-prone environments.

Radar level sensors and guided wave radar level sensors use radar pulses to measure the distance to the liquid surface or guided along a probe, respectively. These non-contact sensors are suitable for a wide range of liquids, including those with foams, vapors, or dust, and are applicable in high-temperature and high-pressure environments.

The selection of the appropriate level sensor depends on factors such as the type of liquid or solid being measured, the desired accuracy, the environmental conditions, and the specific application requirements. By understanding the strengths and weaknesses of each method, industries can make informed decisions and choose the most suitable level sensor to ensure efficient process control, inventory management, and prevent overflows or underfills.

Float, Ultrasonic, Pressure, and Radar level transmitters

Current Sensors:

Analog amperage sensors, also known as current sensors or "CT", measure the amount of electric current flowing through a circuit. They provide continuous current data, enabling PLCs to monitor electrical loads, detect faults, and control current levels in electrical systems.

In motor control systems, current sensors are employed to monitor the current drawn by electric motors, enabling the detection of anomalies and preventing motor overloads. They play a vital role in power distribution systems, helping monitor current levels in electrical panels and distribution boards to detect potential faults or overloads promptly.

Energy management systems benefit from current sensors, which aid in monitoring power consumption and optimizing energy usage in industrial facilities.

Current sensors are critical in ground fault detection systems, identifying and isolating ground faults in electrical systems to prevent hazards and damage, and play a significant role in power monitoring applications by gathering data on power consumption trends, peak loads, and power quality. This information allows for optimized power distribution and energy efficiency improvements.

Voltage Sensors:

Analog voltage sensors measure the electrical potential difference between two points in a circuit. They provide continuous voltage data, allowing PLCs to monitor power supply levels, detect voltage variations, and control voltage levels in electrical systems.

They are employed in a wide range of settings to ensure efficient process control, equipment protection, and safety compliance. In power distribution systems, voltage sensors continuously monitor voltage levels in electrical panels and distribution boards, detecting potential issues like overvoltage or undervoltage conditions to prevent equipment damage.

In motor control systems, voltage sensors play a vital role in monitoring the voltage supplied to electric motors. They detect voltage fluctuations that may impact motor performance, contributing to optimal motor operation and protection. Voltage sensors are also significant in power quality analysis, monitoring and analyzing voltage variations such as sags, swells, and harmonics, allowing industrial facilities to address power quality issues promptly.

Energy management systems benefit from voltage sensors as they help optimize voltage levels, leading to energy efficiency improvements and reduced power consumption. Additionally, voltage sensors are essential for electrical safety, detecting high-voltage conditions or voltage leaks to trigger alarms and isolate circuits when abnormal voltage levels are detected.

Transformers are monitored using voltage sensors to measure voltage on both primary and secondary sides, allowing for assessment of transformer performance and timely detection of issues.

Analog inputs play a crucial role in converting real-world physical parameters into digital values that PLCs can process and use for control decisions. By continuously monitoring temperature, pressure, flow rate, level, amperage, and voltage, PLCs ensure efficient and safe operation of industrial processes and equipment, optimizing performance and maintaining safety standards.

Analog Outputs (Valves, Motors, VFD)

Analog outputs in industrial applications are extensively used to control and regulate devices such as valves, motors, and Variable Frequency Drives (VFDs). These outputs generate continuous signals, typically in the form of voltage or current, to precisely adjust and modulate the behavior of these devices, contributing to efficient process control and automation. Here's a closer look at how analog outputs are utilized in each of these components:

Valves:

Analog outputs are connected to the valve actuators to regulate the valve's position, allowing for precise control of fluid or gas flow rates. By adjusting the analog output signal, operators can accurately control the valve's opening, which directly affects the flow rate. This capability is crucial in applications that require precise control of fluid or gas flow, such as in chemical processes, water treatment, and HVAC systems. Typically the analog output is a 4-20 mA signal transmitted to the valve using a PID instruction to control valve position, if the valve is pneumatic the electrical signal is converted to a proportional

3-15 psi air signal.

Pneumatic and Motorized Valves

Motors:

Analog outputs are instrumental in motor control systems, where they are connected to motor drives or controllers. By varying the analog output signal, the voltage and frequency supplied to the motor can be adjusted, allowing for precise control over the motor's speed, torque, and direction. This level of control is essential in various industrial applications, such as conveyor systems, pumps, fans, and manufacturing processes, where precise motor operation is necessary for optimal performance and energy efficiency.

Industrial Motor

Variable Frequency Drives (VFDs):

Analog outputs are directly related to VFDs, which are devices used to control the speed and torque of AC motors. VFDs convert the analog output signal into variable frequency and voltage output, enabling smooth and precise control over motor speed. This is particularly valuable in applications where varying motor speed is required, such as in pump systems, fans, and conveyors. VFDs provide significant energy savings by adjusting motor speed based on the actual process demand, rather than running the motor at a constant speed.

VFD

5

PLC Data Handling and Memory

PLCs possess data handling capabilities and various memory types to manage and process information in industrial automation. They utilize RAM for temporary storage of data during program execution, ROM for storing the PLC's firmware and program, and EEPROM for retaining user-defined data across power cycles. The PLC supports various data types, such as Boolean, Integer, Real, String, Timers, and Counters, to handle different types of information.

Data handling in PLCs is facilitated through built-in instructions, including data transfer, comparison, arithmetic, and logical instructions. These allow for moving, comparing, and performing mathematical or logical operations on data within the PLC program. PLC memory is organized into specific data tables, such as the Input Table (I) for input device statuses, Output Table (Q) for output device statuses, Data Table (D) for storing program variables, and File Register (F) for user-defined data.

Optimizing memory usage is crucial for efficient program execution, and PLC programmers must carefully manage data and consider the impact of scan time on system performance. By leveraging their data handling and memory resources effectively, PLCs enable precise control and monitoring of industrial processes, ensuring reliable and robust automation in diverse industrial applications.

Bit, Byte, Word, and Double-Word Data Representation

Bit, byte, word, and double-word are common data representations used in computer systems, including Programmable Logic Controllers (PLCs). They are fundamental units for storing and manipulating data in digital systems. Here's a brief explanation of each data representation:

Bit:

A bit is the smallest unit of data in digital systems, representing a binary value of either 0 or 1. It is the basic building block of all digital information and is used to represent the most basic states in a PLC, such as on/off, true/false, or open/closed.

Nibble:

A nibble is a grouping of four bits, representing a half-byte or 4 binary digits. Nibbles are often used for more compact data representation in computer systems and data communication. In a nibble, each bit can have a value of either 0 or 1, allowing for 16 possible combinations . These combinations can represent decimal numbers from 0 to 15.

Nibbles find various applications in digital systems, especially when dealing with hexadecimal notation, which uses base-16 numbers. In hexadecimal, each digit represents 4 bits (a nibble), making it easier to convert between binary and hexadecimal representations. Additionally, certain processors or communication protocols may use nibbles as a convenient way to encode or transmit data, especially in cases where a full byte is not needed.

Nibble

Binary Coded Decimal

Another usage of the nibble is Binary Coded Decimal or BCD, a numerical representation commonly used in digital systems to encode decimal numbers in binary form. Unlike the pure binary model, where each digit corresponds to a power of 2, BCD uses four binary digits (bits) to represent each decimal digit from 0 to 9.

In BCD, each decimal digit (0 to 9) is represented by a unique four-bit binary code. For example:

Decimal Digit	BCD			
	8	4	2	1
0	0	0	0	0
1	0	0	0	1
2	0	0	1	0
3	0	0	1	1
4	0	1	0	0
5	0	1	0	1
6	0	1	1	0
7	0	1	1	1
8	1	0	0	0
9	1	0	0	1

Binary Coded Decimal

BCD is often used in applications where precise decimal representation is required, such as in digital displays, numerical input devices, and some types of data communication. This format allows for direct conversion between binary and decimal, making it easier to display decimal numbers on binary-based devices or vice versa.

It's important to note that BCD requires four bits for each decimal digit, which can result in inefficient use of memory compared to pure binary representation. As a result, BCD is typically used for applications where the exact decimal representation is critical, and memory constraints are not a primary concern.

Byte:

A byte consists of 8 consecutive bits or two combined nibbles. It is the smallest addressable unit of memory in most computer systems. Bytes can represent values from 0 to 255 in binary and are commonly used to store small data elements, such as characters or integer values.

Each bit in a byte can have a value of either 0 or 1, allowing for 256 possible combinations representing decimal numbers from 0 to 255.

Bytes are widely used for storing and manipulating data in computer systems and are commonly employed to represent characters, integers, and various other data types. For example, a byte can represent a single ASCII character or an integer value ranging from 0 to 255.

In PLC programming, bytes store discrete data, where each bit within the byte represents a specific state or condition. For instance, a byte can keep the status of multiple digital inputs or outputs, with each bit representing the state of an individual input or output.

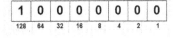

Byte

Word:

A word typically consists of 16 bits, although in some systems, it may be 32 bits or more. Words are used to represent larger data elements and allow for more significant numeric values. For example, a 16-bit word can represent values from 0 to 65,535 in binary. Words are commonly used in PLCs to store integer values, process variables, or control parameters.

Words are used to represent larger data elements and allow for more significant numeric values than bytes. They are commonly employed in various computer operations, such as arithmetic calculations, logical operations, and memory addressing. Words are also used in microcontrollers and PLCs to store and manipulate larger data values, process variables, control parameters, and memory addresses.

Understanding the word size is crucial in programming and optimizing computer systems and PLCs, as it impacts memory usage, data processing speed, and overall system performance. In modern computer architectures, larger word sizes, such as 32-bit or 64-bit, are commonly used to handle complex applications and data-intensive tasks.

1	0	0	0	0	0	0	0	1	0	0	0	0	0	0	0
32,768	16,384	8192	4096	2048	1024	512	256	128	64	32	16	8	4	2	1

Word

Double-Word:

A double-word, also known as a double-word integer or long integer, is twice the size of a word and typically consists of 32 bits. It can represent significantly larger numeric values compared to a word. For example, a 32-bit double-word can represent values from 0 to 4,294,967,295 in binary.

Double-words are commonly used in computer systems and microcontrollers for applications that require handling large numerical values, such as large-scale mathematical calculations, memory addressing, and data-intensive processing tasks. In PLCs, double-words are often used to store and manipulate timestamps, large memory addresses, and significant numeric data, where the standard word size might be insufficient. The choice of word size, whether 32-bit or 64-bit, depends on the specific requirements of the system and the magnitude of the data that needs to be processed or stored.

In summary, bit, byte, word, and double-word are essential data representations in digital systems, including PLCs. They provide a hierarchy of data sizes, with bits representing the smallest unit and double-words representing larger values. Understanding these data representations is crucial for effective data handling and memory management in PLC programming and other digital applications.

IEEE floating-point

IEEE floating-point is a standardized representation for handling real numbers in digital systems, defined by the IEEE 754 standard. It includes three formats: single-precision (32 bits), double-precision (64 bits), and half-precision (16 bits). Single-precision offers a wide dynamic range and reasonable precision, while double-precision provides an even larger range and higher accuracy. Half-precision is the most compact format, suitable for memory-constrained applications.

Each format consists of a sign bit (indicating positive or negative), an exponent, and a significand (also called mantissa). The exponent represents the magnitude of the number, while the significand represents its precision or fractional part. These formats allow for representing a wide range of real numbers, enabling precise arithmetic operations on floating-point data.

IEEE floating-point arithmetic defines rules for performing addition, subtraction, multiplication, and division on floating-point numbers. While it ensures consistent results across different platforms and programming languages, programmers need to be aware of potential rounding errors and precision limitations in extreme cases.

Single-precision and double-precision are commonly used in general-purpose computing and scientific applications where accuracy is crucial. Half-precision finds use in memory-constrained scenarios, such as in embedded systems or graphics processing units, where space efficiency is a priority, and the slightly reduced precision is acceptable.

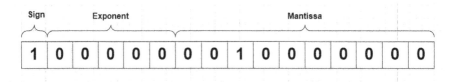

Half Precision Floating Point

Data Registers and Memory Allocation

Data registers and memory allocation are essential concepts in PLC program-ming and digital systems. They play a crucial role in storing, manipulating, and managing data within a PLC's memory. Let's explore each of these concepts:

Data Registers:

Data registers are locations within the PLC's memory that are used to store data temporarily during program execution. They can hold different data types, such as Boolean (for representing true/false values), integers (for whole numbers), floating-point numbers (for decimal values), and strings (for text). Data registers are utilized to store input values, output values, intermediate results of calculations, and various other variables required for PLC operations.

Data registers can be directly accessed and manipulated by the PLC's program instructions, allowing for data processing and decision-making during runtime. PLC programmers must ensure proper usage of data reg-isters, managing memory allocation effectively to avoid unnecessary memory consumption and optimize program performance.

Memory Allocation:

Memory allocation in PLCs involves dividing the available memory into specific areas or data tables for different purposes. Common data tables include:

- **Input Table (I):** Stores the status of input devices, such as sensors and switches.
- **Output Table (Q):** Holds the status of output devices, such as actuators and relays.
- **Data Table (D):** Used for storing program variables, intermediate results, and other data required during program execution.
- **File Register (F):** An additional area for user-defined data, organized in files for specific applications.

Memory allocation is a crucial aspect of PLC programming, as it directly affects the efficiency and performance of the PLC's control and automation tasks. PLC programmers need to manage memory allocation effectively, ensuring that sufficient memory is allocated to each data table while avoiding unnecessary memory wastage. Proper memory allocation also helps prevent memory conflicts and ensures reliable program execution.

In summary, data registers and memory allocation are essential components of PLC programming. Data registers store temporary data during program execution, while memory allocation organizes the PLC's memory into specific areas for input, output, program variables, and user-defined data. Effective management of data registers and memory allocation is critical for optimizing program performance and ensuring successful control and automation of industrial processes.

6

Advanced PLC Programming Techniques

Advanced PLC programming techniques involve the application of sophisticated methodologies to design efficient and precise control systems in industrial automation. Structured programming principles break down complex tasks into manageable modules, ensuring code reusability and easier debugging. Function blocks encapsulate specific functionalities, simplifying program design and promoting modularity.

Data structures and user-defined data types help organize related data elements, enhancing code clarity and facilitating the management of large datasets. State machines enable the automation of sequential processes by modeling different states and transitions. PID control algorithms provide precise and responsive control over industrial processes, minimizing errors and fluctuations.

Advanced HMI integration empowers operators with real-time monitoring, data logging, and visualization, leading to improved decision-making and process control. Communication protocols facilitate seamless data exchange between PLCs and other devices, enhancing information flow and enabling remote monitoring.

Safety programming techniques ensure the reliability and security of industrial operations by implementing safety interlocks, emergency stop procedures, and fail-safe mechanisms. Overall, advanced PLC programming techniques empower engineers to create robust, scalable, and sophisticated control systems, optimizing efficiency, accuracy, and safety in modern industrial automation.

Timers and Counters

Timers and counters are essential components in PLC programming, used to manage time-based operations and event counting in industrial automation applications. They are versatile tools that enable precise control and sequencing of processes. Here's an overview of timers and counters:

Timers:

Timers are used to introduce time delays or control the duration of specific operations. PLC timers can be of two types: On-Delay Timers and Off-Delay Timers. On-Delay Timers start counting time when they receive an input signal, and after the specified time elapses, they activate their output. Off-Delay Timers, on the other hand, start counting time when their input signal goes inactive, and after the specified time elapses, they activate their output.

Timers are crucial in controlling equipment startup and shutdown delays, time-based sequences, and process delays. They allow PLC programmers to introduce controlled pauses between operations, ensuring smooth and safe process transitions.

TON Timer

In the timer ladder below a TON timer will begin timing when the Out1 input is true. The timer will continue timing until the preset time of 1000 millseconds is completed once complete the timer Q output will transition to true setting TonoDn output to true. If the timer input transitions to false before the preset time is completed the timer will stop timing and the elapsed time resets to zero.

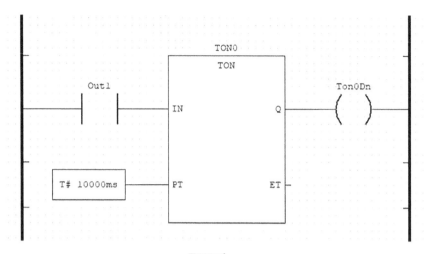

TON Timer

The timing diagram below shows the state of the TonoDn bit transitioning to true when the timer elapsed time is completed.

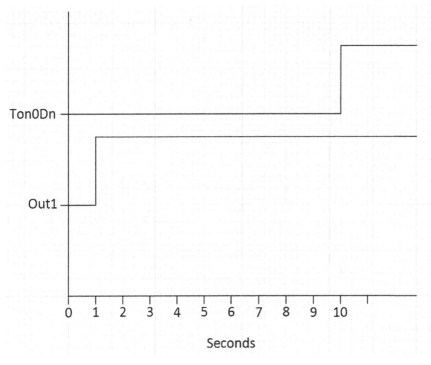

TON Timing Diagram

TOF Timer

In the timer ladder below a TOF timer will begin timing when the Out1 transitions from false to true. The timer will continue timing until the preset time of 1000 millseconds is completed once complete the timer Q output will transition to true setting TofoDn output to true. If the timer input transitions to true before the preset time is completed the timer will stop timing and the elapsed time resets to zero.

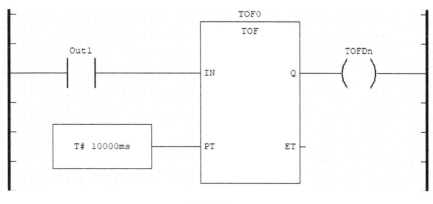

TOF Timer

The timing diagram below shows the state of the TofoDn bit transitioning to true when the timer elapsed time is completed.

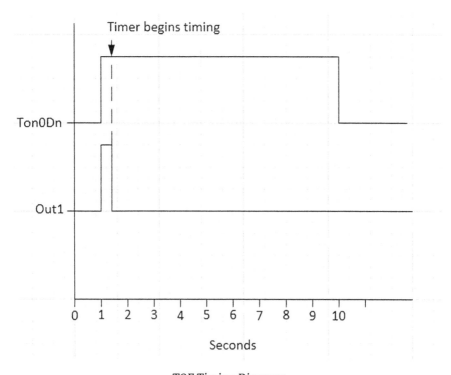

TOF Timing Diagram

Counters:

Counters are used to track the number of events or occurrences of a specific condition. PLC counters can be of two types: Up Counters and Down Counters. Up Counters increment their count value with each input pulse they receive, while Down Counters decrement their count value with each input pulse.

Counters are instrumental in applications that involve event-based control, such as counting the number of products produced, monitoring the number of parts in a manufacturing line, or tracking the number of cycles an equipment undergoes.

CTU Counter

In the counter ladder below each time input CU transitions to true the counter accumulator increments until the count equals the value in the PV. Once the count equals the PV the Q output will energize. when the R input is true the counter will reset.

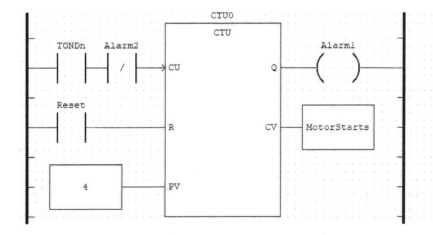

CTD Counter

In the counter ladder below each time input CD transitions false the counter accumulator decrements until the count equals zero. It is important to note that the counter must first be loaded before it can begin decrementing, when the LD input transitions to true the value in the PV will be loaded into the counter accumulator. The CV output displays the current value for the counter accumulator.

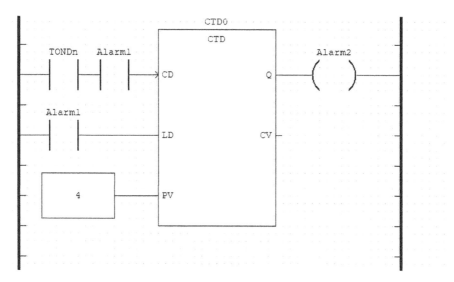

Both timers and counters can be reset manually or automatically, allowing for repetitive or cyclical operations. PLC programmers can use these devices in combination with other control elements, such as relays, contacts, and coils, to create complex control sequences and sophisticated automation logic.

Motor Control and Alarming

Motor control and alarm logic is critical to alert operators of abnormal conditions. While there are many ways to configure alarm logic to monitor motor operation the example given here provides a method that utilizes positive motor running feedback to initiate alarm and shutdown conditions. Building on the motor seal in ladder introduced in chapter 3 this example replaces the Aux contact with the actual motor output coil.

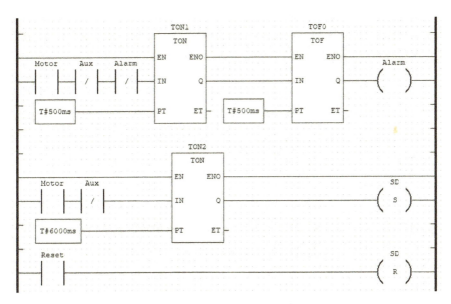

Motor Seal-In

In addition to the change from aux to motor seal-in a shutdown bit SD is added in series to cancel the sealed condition when active. This allows a motor commanded state that remains active until a shutdown is activated.

Alarm and Shutdown logic

In the alarm and shutdown logic above if the motor is commanded to run but is not running the TON/TOF instructions work together to start blinking the Alarm output. If the failure condition exists for 6 seconds a shutdown latch is set true canceling the motor commanded to run condition. The shutdown state will persist until a reset button is pressed unlatching the SD bit.

State Machine

In PLC programming, state engines, also known as state machines, are a valuable design pattern used to manage complex control sequences and automate sequential processes. A state engine represents a system's behavior as a set of well-defined states, where each state represents a specific condition or mode of operation. Transitions between states are triggered by events or conditions, determining the next state to enter.

The implementation of state engines in PLC programming involves the following key components:

- **States**: Each state represents a distinct behavior or mode of the system. States are defined based on the specific requirements of the application. For example, a conveyor system may have states like "Idle," "Running," "Paused," and "Fault."
- **Transitions**: Transitions define the conditions or events that cause the system to move from one state to another. PLC programmers use logical conditions, input statuses, timers, and other triggers to initiate transitions.
- **Actions**: Actions are tasks or operations performed when entering or exiting a state. These actions may involve enabling or disabling specific outputs, setting flags, initiating timers, or performing other control actions.
- **State Diagram**: PLC programmers use a state diagram to visualize the states, transitions, and actions of the state engine. This graphical representation aids in understanding and designing the control logic.

Benefits of using state engines in PLC programming include:

- **Modularity and Reusability**: By breaking down control logic into states and transitions, PLC programmers can create modular and reusable code, simplifying program design and maintenance.
- **Clear Logic Structure**: State engines offer a clear and organized way to represent complex control sequences, making PLC programs more manageable and easier to comprehend.
- **Flexibility and Scalability**: State machines provide a flexible framework that allows for easy modification and expansion of control logic as system requirements evolve.
- **Efficient and Responsive Control**: State engines enable efficient handling of different control sequences, leading to responsive and precise control over industrial processes.

State engines are widely used in PLC programming for applications that involve sequential processes, automating equipment with multiple operating modes, and managing complex control sequences with distinct behaviors. They are an essential tool for creating sophisticated, reliable, and maintainable control systems in industrial automation.

State machine logic is separated into three sections of code, State Register Configuration, State Select Logic , and State Execution Logic these sections can be in the same or different subroutines.

State Diagram

The state diagram below depicts a simple state machine that performs a timed heating and cooling operation with a fault and shutdown condition. In State 0 the state engine is idle and ready for a start command. Once a start command is given the state machine enters state 1 the heating cycle and remains in that state until a preset amount of elapsed time is reached at which time the state engine steps into state 2 for the cooling cycle. After the cooling elapsed time is complete the state engine returns to the heating cycle and continues operating between these two states until a stop or rest command is given or if a fault occurs. Stop or Reset will immediately return the state machine to ready idle.

If a fault occurs in either state 1 or state 2 the state machine switches to state 3 for a set period of time and then begins the shutdown cycle in state 4. If the fault condition clears on its own the Auto Reset is activated returning the state machine to the heating state and the cycle continues.

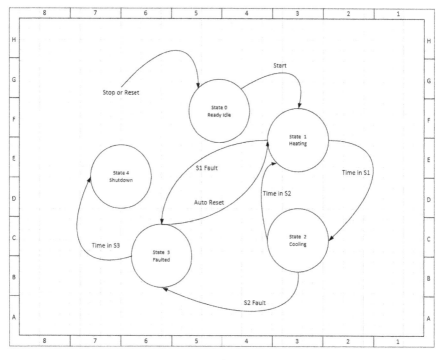

State Diagram

State Register Configuration Logic

The purpose of state register configuration logic is to establish state parameters. In the example we will cover a little later in this chapter there are two basic actions associated with each state transition. When a state is initiated there is a boolean bit that is set to true and remains true as long as the state is selected and a one shot pulse that initiates on state selection. The example below shows the first two states of the state selection logic for a simple state engine, the same pattern is used for as many states as needed.

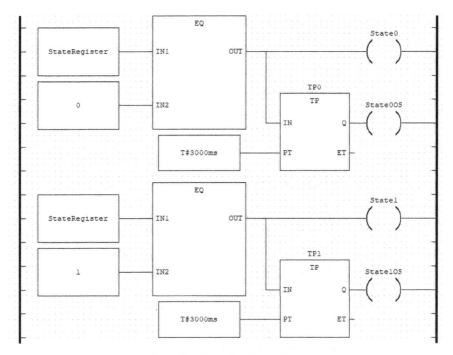

State Register Configuration

Action Logic

Run State

Action logic controls what occurs when a particular state is active. In the example below the run, heating and cooling outputs are set to true if state 1 or 2 is active. Notice we also maintain the run output true even during the fault cycle state 3.

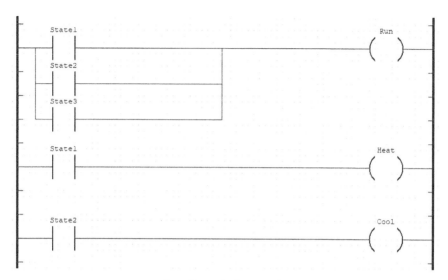

Run State Action Logic

Fault and Shutdown States

If a fault is detected the state engine transitions to state 3 and a TON/TOF timer pair blinks an alarm indicator, if the fault condition persists the state moves into state 4 and a shutdown is activated. The actual transition logic is covered next.

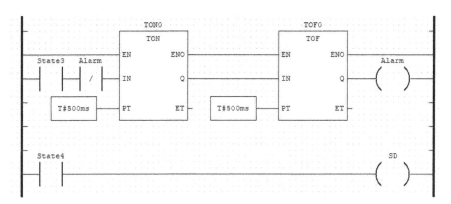

Fault and Shutdown Action Logic

Transition Logic

State Transition

Each state must have logic to move the appropriate state number into the state register such that all transitions are momentary. Any logic that "holds" the value in the state register creates an ambiguous state and may override another section of logic from complicating a stable transition.

State 0: The logic below provides transition logic for State 0, a review of the state diagram will show that only the stop or reset input will move the state machine to state 0.

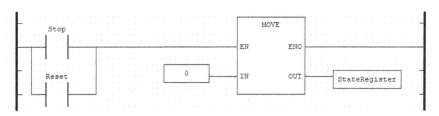

State 0 transition logic

State 1: Referring again to the state diagram only Start, heat command, or auto reset inputs initiate the state 1 transition.

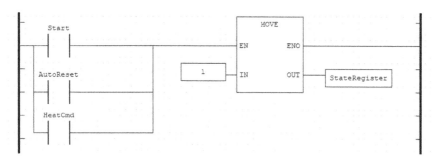

State 1 transition logic

State 2: The only entrance into state 2 cooling is the cooling command input.

State 2 transition logic

State 3: A detected fault moves the state engine into the state 3. Note that the fault detect in a one shot input and does not create a "hold" situation upon the state register. The state register must remain available for other logic transitions, for example if the fault clears the itself the auto reset logic must be able to move the state engine back to state 1.

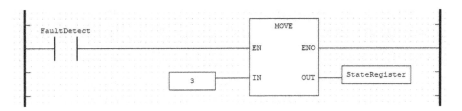

State 4: If the faulted state persists for 10,000 milliseconds a shutdown command is initiated moving the state machine into the final state, state 4. Once the engine has entered the shutdown state there are no exit points for this state and a reset or start command must be issued to re-start the state engine.

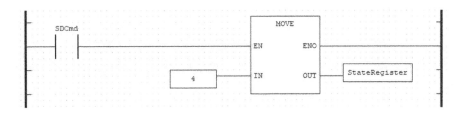

Heating and Cooling

The logic below controls the heating and cooling cycle transitions. When the state engine is in state 1 for 6000 milliseconds the CoolCmd pulse is activated to transitions into state 2. Then 6000 milliseconds later the HeatCmd pulse is activated to transition back to state 1 and this cycle continues as long as there is no fault and run mode is active.

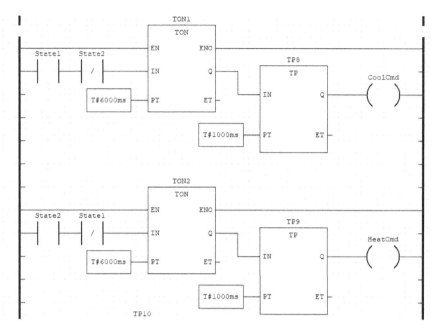

Heating and Cooling Transition Logic

Fault and Shutdown

In the logic below if a fault is detected a pulse is activated to transition the state engine into state 3. At the same time, a timer begins timing and if the fault condition remains for 10,000 milliseconds the state engine transitions to shutdown state 4. The state 1 one shot is included in the timer inputs to reset the fault condition logic in the event the state machine starts when a fault condition is active.

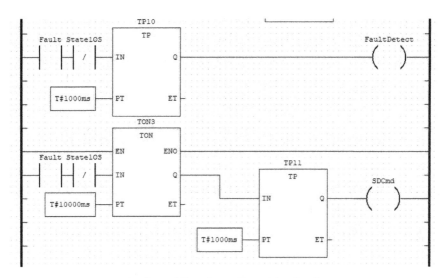

Fault and Shutdown Transition Logic

Auto Reset

If the fault condition clears itself while in the fault state before a shutdown is activated the auto reset pulse will restart the heating cycle returning the state machine to normal operation.

Auto Reset Transition Logic

Closed Loop Control

Closed-loop control, also known as feedback control, is a fundamental concept in engineering and control systems. It is a control mechanism where the system's output is continuously measured and compared to a desired setpoint or reference value. Based on this comparison, an error signal is generated, representing the difference between the desired value and the actual output. The error signal is then used to adjust the system's input or control effort to bring the output closer to the desired setpoint.

The main components of a closed-loop control system are:

- **Process/System:** The physical system or process that needs to be controlled. It can be any dynamic system such as a temperature-controlled oven, a robotic arm, an aircraft's autopilot system, or a chemical reaction in an industrial plant.
- **Sensor/Transducer:** The sensor is a device that measures the actual output or process variable of the system. It provides feedback information to the controller about the current state of the system.
- **Controller:** The controller is the core of the closed-loop control system. It receives the measured output from the sensor and compares it to the desired setpoint. Based on this error signal, the controller calculates the control effort or the input signal to the system. The controller's objective is to minimize the error and maintain the system's output close to the desired setpoint.
- **Actuator:** The actuator is a device that receives the control effort signal from the controller and applies it to the system. It is responsible for making the necessary changes or adjustments to the system's input to achieve the desired output.

The closed-loop control system operates in a continuous feedback loop. As the system runs, the sensor continuously monitors the output, the controller computes the error, and the actuator adjusts the system's input accordingly. This process continues until the system's output converges to the desired setpoint or reference value.

Closed-loop control has several advantages over open-loop control, where the input is determined in advance without considering the system's actual output. Some of the benefits of closed-loop control include:

- **Robustness:** Closed-loop systems are more robust and can handle uncertainties, disturbances, and external variations that affect the system.
- **Accuracy:** By continuously correcting errors, closed-loop control ensures that the system maintains accuracy and stability even in the presence of disturbances.
- **Adaptability:** Closed-loop systems can adapt to changes in the system's behavior over time, making them suitable for dynamic and changing environments.
- **Rejection of Setpoint Changes:** Closed-loop control can quickly respond to changes in the desired setpoint and bring the system to the new target value efficiently.

Closed-loop control is widely used in various fields, including industrial automation, robotics, aerospace, automotive control, and many other applications where precise and stable control of dynamic systems is required.

Proportional-Integral-Derivative Control (PID)

A PID controller, which stands for Proportional-Integral-Derivative controller, is a widely used feedback control mechanism in engineering and industrial applications. It is a type of closed-loop control system that continuously calculates an error signal by comparing the desired setpoint or reference value to the actual output or process variable. The error signal is then used to adjust the control effort (e.g., a control signal or actuator output) to bring the system closer to the desired setpoint.

The three components of a PID controller are as follows:

Proportional (P) Term:

The proportional term is directly proportional to the current error value. It calculates the control effort by multiplying the error with a constant proportional gain (Kp). The greater the difference between the setpoint and the process variable, the larger the control effort applied. The proportional term helps to respond quickly to deviations from the setpoint, but it may lead to steady-state errors if used alone.

Control Effort (u) = Kp * Error

Integral (I) or Reset (R) Term:

The reset term, sometimes denoted as "Tr," accounts for the accumulated error over time in a manner similar to the integral term. However, instead of directly summing the error, the reset term multiplies the error with a constant reset gain (Kr) and then integrates it. This provides similar benefits to the integral term, helping to eliminate steady-state errors and handle system biases.

Control Effort (u) = Kp * Error + Tr * ∫(Error) dt

Derivative (D) Term:

The derivative term remains the same, taking into account the rate of change of the error. It calculates the control effort by multiplying the rate of change of the error with a constant derivative gain (Kd). The derivative term helps to predict the future trend of the error and counteracts abrupt changes, reducing overshoot and oscillations.

Control Effort (u) = Kp * Error + Tr * ∫(Error) dt + Td * d(Error)/dt

By combining these three terms, the PID controller's control effort is determined, and it is continuously applied to the system, helping to maintain the process variable close to the desired setpoint in a stable and efficient manner. The tuning of PID controller gains (Kp, Tr, and Td) is crucial to achieve the desired performance in different systems. Many real-world control systems benefit from the versatility and effectiveness of PID controllers.

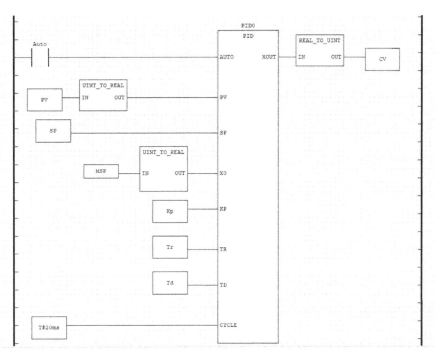

PID Controller Logic

Tuning PID Loops

Tuning PID (Proportional-Integral-Derivative) parameters is a crucial step in implementing a PID controller effectively. Properly tuned PID parameters ensure stable and responsive control of a system, minimizing overshoot, steady-state errors, and oscillations. The tuning process involves adjusting the three gains: Kp (proportional gain), Tr (integral gain), and Td (derivative gain).

Here are some common methods for tuning PID parameters:

Manual Tuning:

This is a basic approach where you adjust each gain manually to achieve the desired performance. The steps are as follows: a. Set Tr and Td to zero initially (disabling integral and derivative control).

1. Increase Kp until the system starts to oscillate.
2. Reduce Kp by approximately 50% to reach the ultimate gain for stability.
3. Slowly increase Tr until steady-state error is minimized but avoid excessive oscillations.
4. Add Td to improve the system's response and dampen oscillations.

Ziegler-Nichols Method:

This is a popular method for tuning PID parameters using the ultimate gain and oscillation period of the system:

1. Set Tr and Td to zero.
2. Increase Kp until the system starts to oscillate at a stable frequency.
3. Measure the ultimate gain (Ku) and the oscillation period (Tu).
4. Use the following formulas to calculate PID gains:

- Kp = 0.6 * Ku
- Tr = 2 * Kp / Tu
- Td = Kp * Tu / 8

Cohen-Coon Method:

This method is based on the system's open-loop step response and provides better results for some systems:

1. Set Tr and Td to zero.
2. Measure the time it takes for the system to reach 63.2% of its final value (t_p) and the time at which the slope of the response is zero (t_o).
3. Use the following formulas to calculate PID gains:

- Kp = (1.35 / Ku) * (t_p / t_o)
- Tr = 2.5 / (Ku * t_o)
- Td = (0.37 * Ku * t_o)

Trial and Error:

In complex systems, trial and error might be the most practical method. Start with conservative gains and incrementally adjust them while observing the system's response. Iterate until satisfactory performance is achieved.

Software Tools and Auto-Tuning:

Some modern control systems provide built-in auto-tuning algorithms or dedicated software tools that can automatically tune PID parameters based on system identification techniques and performance metrics.

Tuning PID parameters can be a time-consuming process, and it requires a good understanding of the system dynamics and control theory. It is essential to test the tuned PID controller under various scenarios to ensure stable and robust performance. Additionally, tuning requirements may change over time due to variations in the system or environmental conditions, so periodic re-tuning might be necessary.

7

PLC Communication and Networking

PLC communication protocols are essential for establishing communication between PLCs and other devices, such as sensors, actuators, HMIs, and other control systems. These protocols facilitate data exchange, control, and monitoring in industrial automation and process control systems. Here's an overview of some commonly used PLC communication protocols:

RS-232 (Recommended Standard 232):

RS-232 is a serial communication protocol that uses a single-ended interface for point-to-point communication. It is characterized by its limited communication distance (typically up to 50 feet) and relatively slow data transmission rates (up to 115.2 kbps). RS-232 is commonly used for connecting PLCs to local HMI devices, laptops, or programming devices.

Modbus ASCII:

Modbus ASCII (American Standard Code for Information Interchange) is another variant of the Modbus protocol. Unlike Modbus RTU (binary representation), Modbus ASCII uses plain ASCII characters to represent data for communication between devices. It is often used over serial communication interfaces like RS-232.

In Modbus ASCII, each byte of data is represented by two ASCII characters, typically in hexadecimal format. This means that the data transmission rate in Modbus ASCII is slower than Modbus RTU, as it requires more characters to represent the same data. Despite its slower data rate, Modbus ASCII has the advantage of being more human-readable when monitoring communication using basic terminal programs.

RS-485 (Recommended Standard 485):

RS-485 is also a serial communication protocol, but it uses a differential signaling method, allowing it to achieve longer communication distances (up to several thousand feet) and support multi-point communication. RS-485 can operate at higher data rates (up to 10 Mbps) and is widely used in industrial applications to connect PLCs with remote I/O modules, sensors, and other peripheral devices.

Modbus RTU:

Modbus RTU (Remote Terminal Unit) is one of the most popular variants of the Modbus communication protocol. It is widely used in industrial automation and process control applications due to its simplicity, efficiency, and faster data transmission rate compared to Modbus ASCII.

Modbus RTU is a binary-based protocol, meaning it uses binary data representation for communication between devices. It operates over serial communication interfaces, such as RS-485, and is known for its reliable and robust performance, making it suitable for communication over long distances in industrial environments.

Ethernet:

Ethernet-based communication protocols are widely used in modern industrial automation. Some popular Ethernet-based protocols used in PLCs include:

Modbus TCP/IP:

Modbus is a widely used protocol for connecting PLCs with various devices over Ethernet. Modbus TCP/IP allows communication between multiple devices, making it suitable for complex control systems.

Ethernet/IP:

Ethernet/IP is an industrial protocol based on standard Ethernet and TCP/IP. It enables real-time communication between PLCs and other automation devices, facilitating seamless integration in EtherNet/IP compatible systems.

PROFINET:

PROFINET is a popular Ethernet-based communication protocol developed by Siemens. It supports real-time data exchange and is widely used in Siemens PLC systems and other industrial automation applications.

EtherCAT:

EtherCAT (Ethernet for Control Automation Technology) is a high-speed industrial communication protocol known for its low communication latency and precise synchronization capabilities. It is often used in applications where tight synchronization and fast communication are critical.

Profibus:

Profibus is a widely used fieldbus communication protocol that allows PLCs to communicate with various devices, such as sensors, actuators, and I/O modules. There are two main types: Profibus DP (Decentralized Peripherals) for fast cyclic communication and Profibus PA (Process Automation) for process automation applications.

Devicenet:

Devicenet is another fieldbus communication protocol commonly used for connecting PLCs with peripheral devices, such as sensors and actuators. It is based on the CAN (Controller Area Network) protocol and offers plug-and-play functionality.

Each of these PLC communication protocols has its advantages and is suitable for different applications based on factors such as distance, data rate requirements, real-time capabilities, and integration with existing systems. Choosing the appropriate protocol depends on the specific needs and constraints of the industrial automation system in question.

Troubleshooting modbus using Modbus Poll

Modbus Poll is a popular software tool used for testing and troubleshooting Modbus communication in industrial automation systems. It allows you to monitor and interact with Modbus devices, read and write data to registers, and check for communication issues. Here are some troubleshooting steps using Modbus Poll:

Check Communication Settings:

Ensure that the communication settings (baud rate, data bits, stop bits, and parity) in Modbus Poll match the settings in the Modbus device and the communication channel you are using (RS-232, RS-485, or Ethernet). Incorrect settings can lead to communication problems. In the example below the target PLC is an ethernet device connected via IP 10.1.10.105 on the standard modbus port 502. Note that the baud rate, data bits, stop bits and parity settings are only used for serial connections.

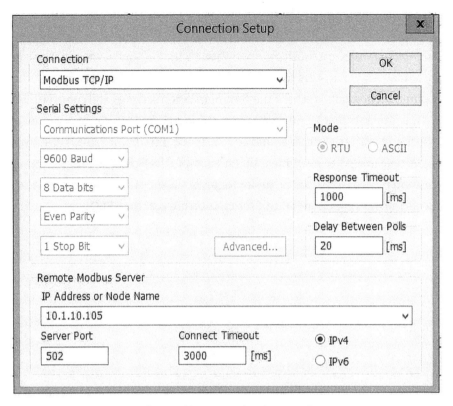

Modbus POll Communications Settings

Verify Device Address:

Ensure that the Modbus device address in Modbus Poll matches the address of the actual Modbus slave device on the network. Modbus devices typically have a unique address assigned to them, and incorrect addressing can lead to communication failures. Typically Ethernet Modbus uses ID 1 or ignores slave ID altogether, determining slave ID is crucial when using Modbus RTU.

Test Communication:

Use Modbus Poll to establish communication with the Modbus device. You can try to read a few registers to verify if the communication is successful. If the communication fails, recheck the communication settings and connections.

Using the state machine example from the last chapter we can examine coils associated with the run,heat and cool outputs. Inputs for fault, start,stop, and reset can also be examined. In our example the OpenPLC programming platform is used to provide examples for program and status. The figure below shows the monitor OpenPLC GUI for monitoring real time PLC data.

Monitoring

Refresh Rate (ms):   100

Point Name	Type	Location	Forced	Value
Start	BOOL	%IX0.3	No	FALSE
Stop	BOOL	%IX0.4	No	FALSE
Fault	BOOL	%IX0.5	No	FALSE
Reset	BOOL	%IX0.6	No	FALSE
Run	BOOL	%QX0.0	No	TRUE
Heat	BOOL	%QX0.1	No	FALSE
Cool	BOOL	%QX0.2	No	TRUE
Alarm	BOOL	%QX0.3	No	FALSE
StateRegister	INT	%MW2	No	2
SD	BOOL	%QX0.4	No	FALSE

OpenPLC State Engine Monitor

The next figure shows the IO data table for the OpenPLC program.

88

#	Name	Class	Type	Location	Initial Value
1	Start	Local	BOOL	%IX0.3	
2	Stop	Local	BOOL	%IX0.4	
3	Fault	Local	BOOL	%IX0.5	0
4	Reset	Local	BOOL	%IX0.6	
5	Run	Local	BOOL	%QX0.0	0
6	Heat	Local	BOOL	%QX0.1	
7	Cool	Local	BOOL	%QX0.2	
8	Alarm	Local	BOOL	%QX0.3	
9	StateRegister	Local	INT	%MW2	0

State Register: The State register is a modbus holding register and can also be monitored using Modbus Poll as shown below:

Tx = 7802: Err = 12: ID = 1: F = 03: SR = 1000ms

	Name	01020	Name	01030
2				0
3				0
4		0		
5		0		
6		2		
7		0		
8		0		
9		0		

viewing State Register using Modbus Poll

The target PLC for this example is OpenPLC running on a Raspberry Pi. The RPI data map for holding registers begins at register 1024, our example uses %MW2 which equates to modbus register 1026. We can see from this table that the state engine is currently in state 2.

Coils: Coils can also be monitored using Modbus Poll as shown below:

Tx = 8596: Err = 13: ID = 1: F = 01: SR = 1000ms

	Name	00000	Name	00010
0				0
1		0		0
2		1		0
3		0		0
4		0		0
5		0		0
6		0		0
7		0		0

Viewing coils using Modbus Poll

The Heating and Cooling state engine uses 4 coils, Run, Heat,Cool, and Alarm. In this example the state machine is cooling in state 2 and the Cool output is true.

Inputs: Inputs are monitored using Modbus Poll as shown below:

	Name	00000	Name	00010
0		1		1
1		1		0
2		1		0
3		0		0
4		0		0
5		0		0
6		0		0
7		0		0

Tx = 7013: Err = 12: ID = 1: F = 02: SR = 1000ms

viewing inputs using Modbus Poll

The state engine uses digital inputs for start, stop, reset, and fault condition. In the example above none of the inputs are currently active, inputs 0-2 are not used in our example.

1. **Check Data Types**: Ensure that you are using the correct data types for reading and writing data in Modbus Poll. Modbus supports different data types (e.g., 16-bit integers, 32-bit integers, floating-point, etc.), so using the wrong data type can result in incorrect data interpretation.
2. **Monitor Responses**: When you read data from the Modbus device, check the responses in Modbus Poll. It will show the data returned by the device. Verify if the data matches the expected values.
3. **Inspect Error Messages**: If there are communication errors or exceptions reported by Modbus Poll, carefully read and analyze the error messages. These messages can provide valuable insights into the root cause of the communication problem.
4. **Check Device Status**: Some Modbus devices have status or diagnostic registers that provide information about the device's health and communication status. Use Modbus Poll to read these registers and look for any

indications of device issues.

5. **Test Write Operations**: If you are having trouble writing data to the Modbus device, use Modbus Poll to write data to specific registers and verify if the changes are applied correctly.

6. **Verify Wiring and Hardware**: If you are using serial communication (RS-232 or RS-485), check the physical wiring and connections. Make sure the devices are properly grounded, and there are no loose or damaged cables.

7. **Refer to Modbus Poll Documentation**: If you encounter any issues or errors that you cannot resolve, consult the Modbus Poll documentation or user guides. The software vendor may provide troubleshooting tips and solutions for common problems.

Remember that Modbus Poll is a diagnostic tool, and it can help you identify communication issues. However, if the problems persist, it may be necessary to inspect the configuration of your PLC, Modbus devices, and other components of your automation system. In such cases, consulting the documentation of your specific devices or seeking support from the equipment manufacturers can be beneficial.

8

Troubleshooting and Debugging PLC Programs

Troubleshooting and debugging PLC programs can be a challenging task, but with the right approach and tools, you can efficiently identify and resolve issues. Here are some essential steps and tips for troubleshooting PLC programs:

Gather Information and Understand the Program:

Before diving into troubleshooting, make sure you have a thorough understanding of the PLC program's logic, its purpose, and expected behavior. Review the program documentation, ladder logic diagrams, function block diagrams, or other programming languages used in the PLC.

The "gather information" stage of PLC troubleshooting is a critical step that lays the foundation for identifying and resolving issues. During this phase, the focus is on collecting relevant data and details to gain insights into the problem at hand.

To begin, technicians and engineers need to clearly define the problem they are facing. This involves understanding what aspect of the PLC system is malfunctioning or behaving unexpectedly. By documenting the symptoms in detail, they can create a clear picture of the issue's nature.

One of the primary sources of information during this stage is error messages displayed by the PLC or its associated software. These messages often provide valuable clues about the underlying cause of the problem, serving as a starting point for further investigation.

Observing the PLC's behavior during runtime is another essential aspect of gathering information. Technicians closely monitor the system's inputs and outputs to identify any abnormal patterns or fluctuations. These observations help them understand the system's actual behavior compared to the expected behavior described in the program documentation.

The team also examines any recent changes made to the PLC program, hardware, or system configuration. These changes might have introduced unintended consequences that triggered the issue. Understanding the sequence of events leading up to the problem can be crucial in resolving it.

Thoroughly reviewing the PLC program documentation is vital to gain insight into the system's intended behavior. Ladder logic diagrams, function block diagrams, and technical specifications help technicians understand how the program should function under normal circumstances.

Throughout the gather information stage, detailed documentation is crucial. A thorough record of the information collected, observations made, and potential causes identified aids in effective analysis and communication during the troubleshooting process. This documentation can also serve as a valuable resource for future reference or for training purposes.

Check Hardware Connections:

Checking hardware connections is a crucial step in troubleshooting PLC issues. Physical connections between the PLC, sensors, actuators, and other devices must be verified to ensure proper functioning of the system.

Begin by inspecting all wiring connections between the PLC and the input/output devices. Look for loose or disconnected wires, damaged cables, or any signs of wear and tear that might affect signal transmission.

Pay special attention to terminal blocks and connectors. Make sure they are securely tightened and free of any contaminants like dust or corrosion that could impede electrical conductivity.

Check for correct wiring polarity, especially in systems that use polarized devices. Incorrect polarity can lead to erroneous input readings or damage to the equipment.

Verify that the sensors and actuators are correctly connected to the PLC's input and output modules, respectively. Ensure that each input corresponds to the correct sensor and each output corresponds to the appropriate actuator.

Inspect power connections to the PLC and other devices to confirm that they are receiving the required voltage and current. Low power supply or voltage fluctuations can cause unpredictable behavior in the system.

When dealing with analog signals, verify the correct scaling and calibration of sensors and actuators to ensure accurate readings and responses.

Take note of any warning or error indicators on the PLC or its modules. These indicators can provide valuable information about faulty connections or module malfunctions.

Perform a visual inspection of the PLC and associated devices to check for any physical damage or abnormalities that might be affecting their performance.

During the hardware check, follow safety procedures and ensure the system is powered off or isolated from hazardous energy sources to prevent accidents.

In complex systems with multiple modules and connections, consider using tools like multimeters or cable testers to validate the integrity of the wiring and connections.

Document your findings and any corrective actions taken during the hardware connection check. Accurate documentation is essential for tracking changes and ensuring consistency in future troubleshooting efforts.

Regularly inspect and maintain the hardware connections to prevent future issues. Dust and debris accumulation can impact performance over time, so periodic cleaning may be necessary.

By thoroughly checking hardware connections, you can rule out potential physical issues that could be causing the problem and focus your troubleshooting efforts on other areas of the PLC system.

Monitor I/O Signals:

Monitoring I/O signals is a critical aspect of troubleshooting PLC programs. Input and output signals play a central role in the operation of the PLC system, and monitoring them provides valuable insights into its behavior.

Use the PLC's monitoring tools or software to observe the status of input devices. Ensure that the PLC is correctly receiving signals from sensors, switches, or other input sources. Verify that the inputs change state as expected when their corresponding conditions are met.

For digital inputs, check for fluctuations in signals when the associated sensors or switches are activated or deactivated. Confirm that the PLC responds promptly and accurately to these changes.

If the system uses analog inputs, observe the values received by the PLC from sensors such as temperature or pressure transducers. Ensure that the readings are within the expected range and respond appropriately to variations in the physical process being monitored.

During the monitoring process, pay close attention to any input signals that remain stuck or show inconsistent behavior. Stuck inputs might indicate a problem with the sensor or the wiring, while erratic signals could be caused by electrical noise or grounding issues.

Next, monitor the output signals of the PLC. Verify that the actuators, such as motors, solenoids, or valves, are being activated correctly in response to the program's logic.

Check the response time of the outputs to ensure they actuate without delay when the corresponding conditions are met. Delayed or sluggish responses might indicate issues with the program logic, timers, or output modules.

For digital outputs, confirm that they toggle between on and off states as intended. For analog outputs, ensure that the PLC is sending the correct scaled values to control the actuators accurately.

If possible, simulate different scenarios to test the PLC's response. Manually force inputs or use simulated input values to trigger various program paths and observe the corresponding outputs.

Keep a close eye on any diagnostic indicators provided by the PLC software or hardware. These indicators can provide real-time feedback on the status of I/O signals and may highlight issues that require attention.

Document the results of the I/O signal monitoring process. Note any abnormalities or discrepancies observed during the testing. These records will aid in further analysis and troubleshooting efforts.

Monitoring I/O signals provides critical feedback on the PLC's interactions with the external world. It helps to verify that the PLC is receiving the correct inputs and generating the desired outputs, allowing you to identify potential problems and refine the troubleshooting process effectively.

Monitoring I/O signals is a critical aspect of troubleshooting PLC programs. Input and output signals play a central role in the operation of the PLC system, and monitoring them provides valuable insights into its behavior.

Use the PLC's monitoring tools or software to observe the status of input devices. Ensure that the PLC is correctly receiving signals from sensors, switches, or other input sources. Verify that the inputs change state as expected when their corresponding conditions are met.

For digital inputs, check for fluctuations in signals when the associated sensors or switches are activated or deactivated. Confirm that the PLC responds promptly and accurately to these changes.

If the system uses analog inputs, observe the values received by the PLC from sensors such as temperature or pressure transducers. Ensure that the readings are within the expected range and respond appropriately to variations in the physical process being monitored.

During the monitoring process, pay close attention to any input signals that remain stuck or show inconsistent behavior. Stuck inputs might indicate a problem with the sensor or the wiring, while erratic signals could be caused by electrical noise or grounding issues.

Next, monitor the output signals of the PLC. Verify that the actuators, such as motors, solenoids, or valves, are being activated correctly in response to the program's logic.

Check the response time of the outputs to ensure they actuate without delay when the corresponding conditions are met. Delayed or sluggish responses might indicate issues with the program logic, timers, or output modules.

For digital outputs, confirm that they toggle between on and off states as intended. For analog outputs, ensure that the PLC is sending the correct scaled values to control the actuators accurately.

If possible, simulate different scenarios to test the PLC's response. Manually force inputs or use simulated input values to trigger various program paths and observe the corresponding outputs.

Keep a close eye on any diagnostic indicators provided by the PLC software or hardware. These indicators can provide real-time feedback on the status of I/O signals and may highlight issues that require attention.

Document the results of the I/O signal monitoring process. Note any abnormalities or discrepancies observed during the testing. These records will aid in further analysis and troubleshooting efforts.

Monitoring I/O signals provides critical feedback on the PLC's interactions with the external world. It helps to verify that the PLC is receiving the correct inputs and generating the desired outputs, allowing you to identify potential problems and refine the troubleshooting process effectively.

Monitoring I/O signals is a critical aspect of troubleshooting PLC programs. Input and output signals play a central role in the operation of the PLC system, and monitoring them provides valuable insights into its behavior.

Use the PLC's monitoring tools or software to observe the status of input devices. Ensure that the PLC is correctly receiving signals from sensors, switches, or other input sources. Verify that the inputs change state as expected when their corresponding conditions are met.

For digital inputs, check for fluctuations in signals when the associated sensors or switches are activated or deactivated. Confirm that the PLC responds promptly and accurately to these changes.

If the system uses analog inputs, observe the values received by the PLC from sensors such as temperature or pressure transducers. Ensure that the readings are within the expected range and respond appropriately to variations in the physical process being monitored.

During the monitoring process, pay close attention to any input signals that remain stuck or show inconsistent behavior. Stuck inputs might indicate a problem with the sensor or the wiring, while erratic signals could be caused by electrical noise or grounding issues.

Next, monitor the output signals of the PLC. Verify that the actuators, such as motors, solenoids, or valves, are being activated correctly in response to the program's logic.

Check the response time of the outputs to ensure they actuate without delay when the corresponding conditions are met. Delayed or sluggish responses might indicate issues with the program logic, timers, or output modules.

For digital outputs, confirm that they toggle between on and off states as intended. For analog outputs, ensure that the PLC is sending the correct scaled values to control the actuators accurately.

If possible, simulate different scenarios to test the PLC's response. Manually force inputs or use simulated input values to trigger various program paths and observe the corresponding outputs.

Keep a close eye on any diagnostic indicators provided by the PLC software or hardware. These indicators can provide real-time feedback on the status of I/O signals and may highlight issues that require attention.

Document the results of the I/O signal monitoring process. Note any abnormalities or discrepancies observed during the testing. These records will aid in further analysis and troubleshooting efforts.

Monitoring I/O signals provides critical feedback on the PLC's interactions with the external world. It helps to verify that the PLC is receiving the correct inputs and generating the desired outputs, allowing you to identify potential problems and refine the troubleshooting process effectively.

LogData:

Logging data is an essential aspect of troubleshooting PLC programs. Data logging involves capturing and recording relevant variables' values during the PLC's runtime. This logged data can provide valuable insights into the system's behavior and help in identifying and resolving issues.

PLC programming software often includes features that allow engineers to specify which variables to monitor and the frequency of data capture. Engineers can select input signals, output signals, internal memory values, timers, counters, or any other critical variables for logging.

The logged data can be stored in various formats, such as CSV files, databases, or memory blocks within the PLC itself. Some PLCs also offer the option to log data remotely to external servers for long-term storage and analysis.

Data logging is particularly useful when troubleshooting intermittent issues or events that occur infrequently. By capturing the data over time, engineers can observe patterns, trends, or triggers that might not be immediately apparent during regular monitoring.

When encountering a problem, engineers can review the logged data to pinpoint the specific conditions or sequence of events leading up to the issue. They can compare the logged values with the expected behavior defined in the program documentation to identify discrepancies.

Logging data also aids in verifying the effectiveness of any applied solutions. Engineers can compare the data before and after implementing a fix to ensure that the problem has been resolved as intended.

It is essential to log data for an appropriate duration, depending on the nature of the issue and the available memory or storage capacity. Logging data for extended periods may require careful management of memory resources.

While data logging is a valuable tool for troubleshooting, it is crucial to log only the necessary variables to avoid overwhelming the system and consuming excessive memory or processing power.

Divide and Conquer:

The "Divide and Conquer" approach is a problem-solving strategy often employed during PLC troubleshooting. It involves breaking down a complex problem into smaller, more manageable parts to isolate and identify the root cause of the issue.

When faced with a large and intricate PLC program, attempting to troubleshoot the entire system at once can be overwhelming and time-consuming. By dividing the program into smaller sections or logic blocks, engineers can focus their efforts on specific areas and analyze them independently.

Here's how the "Divide and Conquer" strategy works during PLC troubleshooting:

Identify Sections:

Begin by identifying distinct sections or modules within the PLC program. These sections may correspond to different machine operations, specific functions, or subsystems.

Isolate Problematic Section:

If there is an issue with the PLC system, try to isolate the specific section where the problem occurs. By narrowing down the scope, engineers can concentrate their attention on a smaller portion of the program.

Verify Inputs and Outputs:

Once a problematic section is identified, verify the inputs and outputs related to that section. Check the signals, sensor readings, and output activations to ensure they are working as intended.

Check Logic and Data:

Review the logic used in the isolated section. Look for potential errors in the ladder logic, function block diagrams, or other programming language used. Verify data manipulation and calculations within that section.

Test Independently:

Depending on the PLC programming software and hardware, engineers may have the option to test the isolated section independently. Simulate inputs or manually force inputs to observe how the program responds within that specific section.

Observe Interactions:

Examine the interactions between the isolated section and other parts of the PLC program. Identify how data is passed between different modules and assess the impact of the isolated section on the overall system.

Iterative Process:

If the issue is not immediately apparent, engineers may need to repeat the process, dividing the section further into smaller blocks until they pinpoint the exact location of the problem.

By dividing the problem into smaller pieces and examining them individually, engineers can efficiently narrow down the source of the issue. This approach not only simplifies troubleshooting but also facilitates collaboration among team members, as different individuals can focus on specific sections simultaneously.

Once the root cause is identified in the isolated section, engineers can focus their efforts on resolving the issue within that particular segment of the PLC program. The "Divide and Conquer" approach is a powerful method that helps streamline troubleshooting and accelerates the resolution of PLC-related problems.

Check for Logic Errors:

Review the logic of the program for any potential errors, such as incorrect use of timers, counters, or mathematical operations. Carefully inspect the ladder logic, compare it with the intended behavior, and look for unintended consequences.

Test Inputs and Outputs:

Simulate inputs or manually force them to test how the PLC responds. Similarly, test outputs by verifying if the correct actuators are activated as expected.

Use Online Debugging:

Some PLC programming software allows online debugging, enabling you to monitor and modify the program while it's running. Use this feature to trace the program execution and identify potential issues.

Read PLC Status Indicators:

Most PLCs have status indicators (e.g., LEDs) that provide information about the system's state. Pay attention to these indicators for any patterns or anomalies.

Check Error Codes and Diagnostics:

PLCs often provide error codes and diagnostic messages. Refer to the PLC's user manual or documentation to interpret these codes and understand the nature of the issue.

Firmware and Software Updates:

Ensure that the PLC's firmware and programming software are up to date. Sometimes, updating the software can resolve known issues.

Review Changes:

If the problem occurred after a recent modification to the program or system, review the changes made and their potential impact.

Collaborate with Others:

Don't hesitate to seek help from colleagues or experts who have experience with PLCs or similar systems. Fresh perspectives can sometimes lead to quicker solutions.

Backup the Program:

Before making any significant changes to the PLC program, create a backup to avoid losing the original working configuration.

Remember to be patient and methodical while troubleshooting PLC programs. Document your steps and findings, as this information can be valuable for future reference or when training others.